DRAWING/
ESSAYS IN AR

ANDREA KAHN, EDITOR

PRINCETON ARCHITECTURAL PRESS
NEW YORK

Princeton Architectural Press, Inc.
37 East 7th Street
New York, New York 10003
212.995.9620
ISBN 0-910413-71-1

©1991 Princeton Architectural Press, Inc.
and the authors.
Printed in the United States of America
94 93   5 4 3 2
Book design: Kevin Lippert
Production editor: Clare Jacobson
Special thanks to Sheila Cohen, Scott Corbin,
Antje Fritsch, Stefanie Lew, and Ann Urban.

Library of Congress CIP data
Drawing/building/text: essays in architectural theory
Andrea Kahn, editor.
175 pp.   5 3/4" x 9 1/4"
ISBN 0-910413-71-1: $14.95
1. Architecture—Philosophy. I. Kahn, Andrea, 1958–
NA2500.D7   1991   91-23014
720'.1—dc20   CIP

THIS PROJECT WAS SUPPORTED BY A GRANT
FROM THE GRAHAM FOUNDATION FOR
ADVANCED STUDIES IN THE ARTS.

Contents

Andrea Kahn	Foreword	5
Miriam Gusevich	The Architecture of Criticism A Question of Autonomy	8
Peggy Deamer	Subject/Object/Text	25
Jennifer Bloomer	Toward Desiring Architecture Piranesi's *Collegio*	43
Catherine Ingraham	Lines and Linearity Problems in Architectural Theory	63
Andrea Kahn	The Invisible Mask	85
Ann Bergren	Baubo and Helen Gender in the Irreparable Wound	107
Mary Pepchinski	The Landscape of Memory	127
Carol Burns	On Site Architectural Preoccupations	146
Lois Nesbitt	Postscript	168
	Figure Credits	171
	Author Biographies	174

ANDREA KAHN

EDITOR'S FOREWORD

While those works commonly recognized as architecture are indisputably located on limited sites, the boundaries of the discipline of architecture are remarkably difficult to situate. In the physical world, architecture builds distinctions between here and there, inside and outside, accessibility and inaccessibility. It defines spatial limits, creates material enclosures. In so doing, architecture manifests conceptual enclosures as well. As a praxis, architecture determines a means of inquiry and research; it inscribes the limits of its own field of activity.

This volume was conceived as a speculation on the discipline of architecture—what we think it is, what we make of it, how we make through it. Positing architectural work in both material and conceptual processes, the essays assembled here aim to identify architecture's positions—its locations as well as its points of view, its *site* as well as its *program*. On one hand, the collection represents an attempt to approach architecture architecturally—that is, it tries to assemble diverse and often divergent claims into a coherent construction. On the other hand, it questions what exactly an architectural "approach" might be.

Architectural schemes: challenges posed by the forces shaping architectural production as well as architecture's own testing of those constraints provide its material. When its myriad aspects are brought together the result resembles less a unified territory than a place of intersections, overlaps, and gaps. What appears is a site of joints—inscribed between architecture's "proper" forces (theoretical, historical, professional, formal, etc.) and between these and circumstantial forces exerted by the "world at large" (political, cultural, economic, aesthetic, etc.). Each stakes a claim on the discipline, and it is the work of architecture to project the terms of their contesting interests.

As the title of this volume implies, architecture is here understood to encompass texts and drawings as well as buildings, and the discipline of architecture is instituted by and erected between these three modes of production. Joints are elemental connections that accommodate differences in the service of holding things together. Their materials are at once independent and interdependent aspects of a construction. The design of joints involves making decisions as to which materials will create stable connections. This process is similar to that of putting together a discourse or a discipline or, for that matter, a book. There are, however, some significant differences. The choices involved in designing a material joint are physically and visually motivated, based on ideologically neutral factors for example, capacities for expansion and contraction. Conversely, the choices made in the formation of a discipline and its discursive constructions are always politically motivated, based on assumptions about what is and is not within the bounds of a given field of knowledge.

An anthology introduces yet another selection process—the choice of contributors. In this case in particular, the choice of authors—all women—will probably not go unnoticed, despite current claims to a broadened architectural constituency. It was not, however, the result of a predetermined program but reflects decisions taken in the course of the project, choices made as the book took shape. More importantly, the selection of authors arose from my desire to present a collection advocating neither a singular critical methodology nor a unified critical stance. The compilation is meant to accentuate the multivalent nature of architectural work. Whereas a structural joint is designed to insure stability, the current work of joinery is designed to promote the opposite condition. These writings destabilize certain assumptions limiting our conception of the discipline, disclose new territory rather than enclose an existing site.

"The politics of disciplinization, conceived as all disciplinization must be, as a set of negations, consists in what it marks out for *repression* for those who wish to claim the authority of discipline itself for their learning,"[1] Hayden White has written regarding history. Even if negation and repression are preconditions of disciplines, the

---

1. Hayden White, "The Politics of Historical Interpretation: Discipline and De-sublimation," in *Critical Inquiry*, vol. 9, no. 1 (September 1982): 119.

criteria determining what is included or excluded from disciplined architectural praxis can and must always remain open to question. In the broadest sense, the topic of this volume is architecture's disciplinary politics. The collection originated in a series of questions sent to the contributors:

> How do inter/intra-disciplinary relationships contribute to a conception of the limits of the field of architecture?
> What is the relative status of drawn, built, and textual production, and how do these aspects of the discipline interact?
> Are there multiple architectures?
> Do they engender exclusive realms of discourse?
> Do they lead to exclusionary audiences and constituencies?
> How do the assumptions circumscribing the context and concerns of contemporary architectural discourse effect the structure of architecture as a field of knowledge?

The purpose of these questions was to approach architecture at various scales simultaneously, to contemplate its materials, and to assess its constraints—in essence to question the program of the discipline. Predicated upon the belief that architecture is a speculative process and open to critical self-questioning, the questions were meant to provoke and did indeed prompt provocative, if indirect, responses. Together, the eight essays create a web of oblique connections, transparencies, and contradictory positions suggesting many different figures. I have tried to attend to different scales and multiple readings, organizing the pieces around points of intersection *and* points of contention, since architecture is perhaps most accurately described by its simultaneous yet incommensurate concerns—perhaps it is only known through its conflicted interests.

There are, of course, many possible paths across and amidst the eight texts and, in the end, a collection like this can only be approached through its individual authors. Above all, it is to them and to Lois Nesbitt for her postscript that I extend my deepest thanks and appreciation. Additional thanks go to Lois for her insightful and constructive editorial assistance, not to mention her undying enthusiasm for the project; to Kevin Lippert at Princeton Architectural Press for his help and his support; and finally, to my friends, especially Carol, Clem, and Graham, who never let me lose my sense of humor.

Miriam Gusevich

The Architecture of Criticism:
A Question of Autonomy

The architect is a builder who has learned Latin.—Adolf Loos

Architecture and Building

The term "architecture" is of Greek and Latin provenance; "building," on the other hand, has Anglo-Saxon roots. In common parlance both have the same referent (structure, construction, edifice); they are synonyms. Nevertheless, they have different connotations, architecture meaning something superior to building.[1]

We confront the paradox of a binary structure that is simultaneously equivalent and hierarchical, where the two terms are identical yet opposite, with one (architecture) dominating the other (building).[2] This paradox can be resolved if we recognize that "architecture" refers to two different and incommensurable conditions. Architecture equals building when referring to the artifact, the object for human habitation, or the craft of construction; it is unequal to building when referring to the canon, meaning "an enduring exemplary collection of books, buildings, and paintings authorized (by criticism) for contemplation, admiration, interpretation, and the determination of value."[3]

The architectural canon is an effect of criticism, which institutionalizes the difference between architecture and building. Historically, the difference was clearly established: architecture referred to monuments and building to "common" structures. Monuments (i.e. churches and palaces) were constructed through the exercise of power and represented, celebrated, and glorified that power. Architecture, then, represented the elite; it spoke Latin, the language of the Church and of the court. Thus the claim of superiority of architecture as monument was supported implicitly by the claim of social superiority that it housed and represented. The canon constituted an aristocracy or meritocracy of built form paralleling the social aristocracy of blood.[4] Any traditional architectural history book such as Bannister Fletcher's *History of Architecture* reveals how the architectural canon was defined exclusively in elite terms.[5]

Any book on modern architecture presents a different spectacle.[6] Churches and palaces are rare. Instead, one discovers factories (e.g. Peter Behrens's AEG Factory, Walter Gropius's Fagus Factory) schools, hospitals, museums, and private houses, by Le Corbusier, by Richard Neutra, by Alvar Aalto, etc. In light of the previous distinction between architecture and building, this selection of "ordinary" buildings is really quite remarkable and, on reflection, even baffling. Only familiarity encourages us to take it for granted.

In modern, secular, bourgeois culture buildings continue to represent elite institutions. Instead of churches and palaces there are banks, insurance companies, stock exchanges, museums, universities, schools, and hospitals. The canon still exists, but specific buildings are not included because of type or institutional status, but because they have received critical acclaim.

To cite an example: Le Corbusier's Villa Savoye at Poissy (1929-31) looms very large in the architectural landscape, out of proportion to its actual size or urbanistic importance. In contrast, the Chrysler Building by William Van Allen (1928-30) and the Empire State Building by Shreve, Lamb and Harmon, (1931) were not included in the canon until quite recently despite their size, urban impact, sophisticated use of modern technology, and popularity as modern landmarks.[7]

Villa Savoye shines in the virtual space established by criticism; a space achieved by decontextualizing the object—removing it from the specificity of its social, political, cultural, and sometimes even physical context—and recontextualizing it as a "representation" to be judged on different, specifically "aesthetic" terms. This distinctive operation has informed modern aesthetics at least since the time of Emmanuel Kant, who, in *The Critique of Judgment*, explicitly described its purpose and modus operandi:

> "If anyone asks me whether I consider that the palace I see before me is beautiful, I may perhaps reply that I do not care for things of that sort which are merely made to be gaped at. Or I may reply in the same strain as the Iroquois sachem who said that nothing in Paris pleased him better than the eating

houses. I may even go a step further and inveigh with the vigour of a Rousseau against the vanity of the great who spend the sweat of the people on such superfluous things . . . All this may be admitted and approved, only it is not the point now at issue. All one wants to know is whether the mere representation of the object is to my liking."[8]

This virtual space created by criticism is nonetheless real since it has a definite effect: the buildings included in the canon function as paradigms for subsequent practice.[9]

How does criticism establish the dominant canon? In other words, what are the criteria by which particular buildings ascend to the status of architecture? A primary criterion for inclusion in the architectural canon is aesthetic merit. The most orthodox statement of architectural aesthetic is Vitruvius's trilogy: firmness, commodity, and delight.[10]

Yet aesthetic merit is not the only criterion at work. Many buildings receive critical attention despite—maybe even because of—their questionable aesthetic merit, because they are paradigmatic, exemplary of a particular position or intellectual claim. An instructive historical example is William Butterfield's All Saints, Margaret Street, Westminster, London (1850–59). To Butterfield's contemporaries All Saints was a controversial building: "There is here to be observed the germ of the same dread of beauty, not to say the same deliberate preference of ugliness, which so characterizes in fuller development the later paintings of Mr. Millais and his followers,"[11] an admiring critic wrote in *The Eclesiologist*, the magazine of the Cambridge Camden Society. He praised neither the church's beauty nor its elegance and refinement, but the cultural values represented by its ugliness—the values of the Camden Society that commissioned the church.

An analogous rationale applies to current projects. Robert Venturi's Guild House and Stanley Tigerman's Daisy House are instructive in this regard. Both are relatively modest structures built with standard methods of construction and resembling conventional housing. They are significant for their intellectual claims: Guild House represents Venturi's endorsement of the ordinary à la Pop Art, and Daisy House represents Tigerman's call for humor and irony in architecture. The Guild House is purposefully banal and ordinary; its rear facade is barely distinguishable from that of many low income housing projects of the late 1960s. Daisy House, with its phallic plan, makes explicit reference to Claude-Nicolas Ledoux's House of Pleasure, and aggressively flaunts "good taste." The merit of these examples does not reside in their beauty, craftsmanship, or other conventional criteria of aesthetic judgment. On the contrary, despite these buildings' ordinary appearance, they are significant because they challenge established norms of propriety; they *transgress* the decorum of modern architecture.[12] Ironically, their architects adopt the historical avant-garde's strategy of confrontation, its posture of *épater le bourgeois*, to criticize the avant-garde's aesthetic preference for spartan minimalism. Instead, they reassert the bourgeois preference for comfort and easy accessibility. This paradox is compounded when we recognize that despite the populist claims justifying the architects' aesthetic choices, the cultural significance of these buildings is established through erudition, in a very elite context. To the ordinary citizen, these building would seem fairly ordinary. They appeal instead to the cognoscenti who, aware of the difference between the codes "modern" and "postmodern," can understand and appreciate the intended transgression.

The significance and status of a building as architecture is not dependent on some preestablished set of attributes, on some essential features, but on its status as a cultural object established through critical discourse. This does not deny the importance of aesthetic criteria but stresses their historical specificity, the fact that architectural judgments do not occur in a vacuum, but in particular times, places, and under specific circumstances.[13] In modern times, the relevant criteria, the context, and the purpose of aesthetic judgement have changed. We are witnessing a redefinition of architecture. If architecture traditionally provided the spatial representation of dominant institutions, in modern times architecture houses institutions and yet critiques dominant expectations and values.

Criticism defines architecture as distinct from building and, in recent years, selects paradigms of its capacity to provide a cultural critique. While criticism might not seem necessary to actually build, it is crucial to the act of establishing architecture as a cultural institution. For this reason, it is instructive to explore the interdependence of architecture and criticism.

CRITICISM

Architectural criticism is a privileged discursive practice. This practice is not ad-hoc. It has its own architecture: a site, agents, and a set of governing conventions. Together these features frame criticism as an institution.

Criticism operates in the public realm and so differs from mere opinion or sheer gossip. This public world is a discursive space, constituted by forums such as books, magazines, symposia, conferences, seminars, and, of course, juries, distinctive institutions in the worlds of art and architecture. In recent years this site has dramatically expanded through the proliferation of books and journals and, more remarkably, through the discovery of architecture by the electronic media, especially television. The expansion is due in part to the new popularity of architecture and the media's recognition of the previously untapped market of architectural fans. It is a positive development providing a long overdue acknowledgment of the cultural importance of architecture and urbanism; yet it could have drawbacks if it reduces the public space of discourse to a commodity subject to market pressures.

Criticism's site is not randomly scattered through its constituent forums. The events, texts, and media that comprise this realm have the capacity to structure architectural practice because they are themselves structured hierarchically, following the pattern of their target audience. At the top are journals for the cognoscenti; at the bottom are journals for mass circulation. Each section of the market has a high end that is more intellectual, artistic, and less profitable and a low end that is pragmatic and profitable. The greatest prestige is assigned to the most theoretical, intellectually demanding, and therefore most exclusive publications having the smallest circulation and the most knowledgeable and specialized audience—usually a small community of scholars, critics, and students. In the United States, their most likely home is the academy.[14] Second in line are the professional journals, which address a range of professional concerns from design to business and construction issues.[15] Down the line are the journals for mass circulation.[16] Prestige and profitability are inversely proportional and the relationship of prestigious to profitable journals is unstable and highly contested, reflecting the ongoing struggle between cultural capital and economic capital.[17] The economic power of a profitable publication rests squarely on its ability to reach a large audience, whereas the cultural power of a prestigious publication is more subtle, stemming from the intangible ability to define the canon. Architectural criticism operating in any of these public forums becomes an institution and acquires the power to shape public opinion.

Clearly, not everyone is an equal participant in this process, opinions are not of equal weight, not everyone counts. Architectural discourse is the discourse of an elite who is authorized (as an author is authorized) to present its concerns to the public. In practice, we recognize the members of this elite: renowned architects and journalists, academics and other intellectuals. These professional critics are qualified to speak on the basis of training and professional status, in other words, on the basis of their cultural capital. To the professional critic we may contrast the amateur critic whose opinions are of general public interest not on the basis of technical expertise but of wealth and/or social status—in other words, of economic and social capital (e.g. Donald Trump and Prince Charles). There are significant tensions between these two groups and since they occupy different positions in the social space, they are likely to have a different perspective on architecture.

From the perspective of the professional architect, the man/woman of action, criticism seems a marginal activity, at best a supplement to the central activity of building. Such professionals are ambivalent about the role of the critical establishment; longing for the prestige and status that criticism confers they seek to be recognized and go to great lengths and considerable expense to be published. Yet architects are also suspicious of the power exercised by criticism. The world of architectural production presents an increasingly agonistic site, with architect/producers competing for commissions, contesting the values and expectations of the clients upon whose capital and good will they depend, and acting in uneasy alliance with critics who represent and articulate the interests of architecture as an institution.

Architectural criticism as a discursive practice is governed by a tacit set of rules or conventions that establish the code of propriety. These conventions frame what is permissible and what must not be said; in doing so they govern the shape of architectural criticism which, like the conventions themselves, is subject to historical transformation.[18] In modern times the dominant form of commentary on architecture is the illustrated essay; in the nineteenth century it was illustrated by engravings, now most likely by photographs and a few drawings, usually plans (sectional drawings are rare in American journals). Of increasing although unacknowledged importance is the photo-essay, consisting of photographs with captions. We may also include here the carica ture. All of these are print media, and all are mixed media, incorporating both visual and verbal information. This mixture reproduces within the structure of the essay the problem of translation from non-discursive to discursive structures intrinsic to artistic and architectural criticism.[19]

Film and (more recently) video have brought us the documentary essay; so far this has exploited fairly conventional historical narratives but the medium offers as yet unexplored formal possibilities. Such new developments could be of great significance, since the conventions governing the form of the commentary are related to those establishing the code of propriety. To underscore this relation between the code of propriety and the mode of criticism we may compare the relatively modern critical essay with past modes of commentary. Historically, architectural supplements took many different forms: paintings celebrating the completion of the building, coins, poems, songs. In these cases architectural commentary was usually laudatory, a panegyric congratulating the patron on his wisdom and good judgment. They were commissioned by the patron and were meant to flatter him or her and to promote his or her interests. A standard feature of courtly culture, this laudatory style of commentary survives to this day in some "journalistic" criticism so enthusiastic, so rhapsodic in its appreciation of the architecture that it collapses critical distance, coming dangerously close to propaganda or advertising.

The critical essay, in contrast, might actively contest the values and assumptions of the client who commissioned the building. This form of essay presupposes *critical* distance—critical in the sense of both a censorious judgement and a crucial or decisive condition.[20] This critical distance rests on the independence of the critic from direct patronage, an independence made possible by the anonymity of the market, by protection from censorship, and by academic freedom.[21] The degree of critical distance determines a qualitative distinction among various modes of architectural discourse; these we may distinguish as scholarly commentary, criticism, and critique.

Scholarly commentary presents itself as straightforward and traditional. It has limited ambitions, serving as a textual supplement to the building and elucidating its purpose and meaning. Many architectural history monographs take this form; they provide background information and describe and analyze the building without necessarily judging it or ranking it in relation to other buildings. Such commentary implicitly endows the building with significance by acknowledging it as a specimen worthy of note and of further study, but it does not necessarily make explicit value judgments. At its best, this kind of commentary is distinguished for its scholarship and erudition. Nevertheless, its understated appraisal underestimates the significance of critical discourse. The act of acknowledging, recording, and processing any artifact through the apparatus of historical methodology and archival research endows it with significance. Yet by withholding explicit value judgments, it does not confront the criteria for establishing significance and, as such, suffers from a lack of self-reflection and self-understanding.

Criticism is riskier than commentary. It is willing to judge and to condemn, to stake out and substantiate a particular position. Serious criticism is not sheer negativity; it is the careful and thoughtful disclosure of dimensions that might otherwise elude us. It is instructive, opening up the depth of intelligence built into the architecture. It is also self-reflective, since it recognizes that to identify a building or an urban complex as worthy of discussion implicitly offers it as a potential candidate to the canon, and criticism takes the responsibility to substantiate its judgment.

By conferring judgment, criticism exercises power. This power works indirectly by effectively establishing the canon; and it works directly by making and undoing reputations. It has human consequences: architects may gain or lose commissions, employees may lose their jobs. Criticism entails responsibility; it calls for discretion and judgement. Nevertheless, following Friedrich Nietzsche,"We must know the right time to forget as well as the right time to remember," and we must consider that to do justice, at times we may need to ignore the possibility of offense and the potential for injury, and be critical without fear of the consequences.[22]

Critique goes beyond serious criticism in the process of self-reflection: it investigates the theoretical foundations of judgment (note that foundation is an architectural metaphor.) If criticism is a reflection on architecture, critique is a reflection on the conditions of criticism. Provocative critiques, like Colin Rowe and Fred Koetter's *Collage City*, and Manfredo Tafuri's *Architecture and Utopia: Design and Capitalist Development, Theories and History of Architecture*, and *The Sphere and the Labyrinth*, operate on many levels simultaneously.[23] They address how the structure of architectural production and criticism has changed historically while recognizing their own historicity. They also acknowledge the problematic relation between criticism and its subject—architecture—by exploring the layers of historic experience that mediate our understanding—or misunderstanding—of the inherited built environment. They recognize the role of ideology in shaping our values, expectations, and aesthetic judgment, and provide critiques of ideology, albeit from radically different political perspectives.

Successful critiques also challenge a simplistic understanding of the relationship among different modes of discourse by encompassing all three: commentary, criticism, and critique. They remind us that while this tripartite schema provides a useful distinction among levels of reflection, it can also be misleading, since clear-cut divisions are hard to find in practice. Essays differ by degree; some emphasize description, others analysis, and still others self-reflection. The choice is a question of judgment of what is appropriate to the object under consideration and to the occasion. An ambitious critique seems pretentious when a simple appreciative comment would suffice.

We should also beware of the hierarchy implied in this classification, with critique as the highest and most desirable form of discourse. The pursuit of critique is no panacea; it has many dangers. Critique, which twice removes itself from its object, is a double process of reflection. It is difficult to sustain reflection on the conditions of architectural production and a dialogue with the work of architecture. Ambitious critiques can be so removed from specific

15

architectural considerations as to risk becoming totally irrelevant to the subject ostensibly discussed. In reflecting on very demanding critical texts these works do not function either as good architectural critique or as insightful philosophical exercises.

Another common danger is eclecticism. While current critical production in architecture is quite learned it is often uncritical of its own presuppositions and goals. It uses critique, rather than engaging in it. If architects designed buildings the way they wrote critiques we would be totally surrounded by undisciplined pastiche. The problem is that architects are impatient with the circularity of self-reflection; they want results, and their forays into theoretical territory are motivated by a desire for practical guidelines to inform design decisions. For these reasons, there is the temptation to borrow indiscriminately from other disciplines.

In recent years, the loss of faith in modern architecture as a program and the discrediting of positivism as "physics envy" have encouraged the pursuit of various theoretical critiques borrowing from other disciplines.[24] We have witnessed the wholesale introduction of continental philosophy—Marxism, critical theory, phenomenology, structuralism, poststructuralism—into architectural discourse. (This continental invasion mirrors in a displaced fashion the previous cultural invasion of the International Style half a century earlier). This can yield some unfortunate pastiches: German ones, like the combination of phenomenology (à la Martin Heidegger) with critical theory (à la Frankfort School) without acknowledging Theodore Adorno's critique of phenomenology in *The Jargon of Authenticity*,[25] and French desserts, more clever and playful, such as the privileging of the linguistic and/or textual models of structuralism that ignore the extent to which the logic of structuralism relies on an architectural metaphor.

Also dubious is the current use of deconstruction as a theory to guide architectural production. Deconstruction in architecture has become identified with complex and tortured forms, and crashing, colliding, violent juxtapositions.[26] I do not deny that this type of architecture is seductive; it offers a perverse appeal and reaffirms an "avant-garde" sensibility. The problem is that it seeks to legitimate an aesthetic preference by using (or abusing) a controversial theoretical posture. Deconstruction as a critique of metaphysics might provide a valuable position from which to develop an architectural critique,[27] but not when uncritically appropriated. Jacques Derrida's "deconstruction" in *White Mythology* challenges the truth-claims of philosophy by disclosing the role of metaphor in the construction of truth.[28] To regard buildings as texts or writing as construction can be a provocative metaphor with which to challenge our preconceptions, but to treat deconstruction literally trivializes the deconstructive hermeneutic motivating the metaphor.

According to Paul Ricoeur, metaphor can be understood as "a categorical transgression, . . . a deviation in relation to a pre-existing logical order, as a disordering in a scheme of classification." The metaphor effects this categorical transgression because its structure incorporates an inherent tension: the "is" of the metaphoric cupola includes both an "is like" and an "is not"— it sustains in tension the ambiguity of meaning.[29] When text and architecture are related metaphorically their relation is ambiguous (architecture is like a text and yet, architecture is not a text). The current appropriation of deconstruction in architecture collapses the tension within the metaphor. In doing so it threatens to erase the significant distinction between discursive—writing—and non-discursive—building—practices and ignores the problem of translation between different media. This collapse is significant since it ignores the difference in status and the effects of these two types of practices. By defying common sense it can be easily dismissed as irrelevant and can reinforce the prejudice against theoretical reflection common in the profession.

These intellectual debates are significant in their own terms and for their cultural implications; they form the architectural canon by establishing criteria for judgment, articulating values and assumptions that inform architectural production, and setting trends and expectations that direct subsequent practice. For these reasons, such debates merit serious scrutiny and criticism.

Among the various theoretical critiques challenging the functionalism of the Modern Movement, one of the most persuasive and productive has developed around the reinterpretation of architectural type and, on this basis, around architecture as an autonomous discipline. This claim of autonomy is one I would like to examine .

A QUESTION OF AUTONOMY

The claim that architecture is autonomous has been invoked in recent criticism, especially in connection with architectural type. The concept of architectural type has long been a significant topic in architectural theory, where it has had various interpretations. Gropius and Le Corbusier defined type in two ways: in relation to modern industrial production and in terms of different programmatic needs for specific institutions—schools, hospitals, housing, factories, etc. Recent, mainly European, critics of this functionalist interpretation have stressed architectural type in relation to the continuity of history and the city. In their critiques, type retains a historical and urban referent.[30] When transferred to the United States, the concept of type has been decontextualized and its implications radicalized by invoking the complete autonomy of architecture.[31]

This is puzzling since architecture is a social art par excellence; it is always in complicity with power more explicitly than any other art. To get anything built, an architect needs clients and a social organization of labor; he/she needs control of capital resources, coordination of different building crafts and knowledge of the set of practices that enables construction. Thus architectural production depends on a complex social, economic, and political matrix.

In addition, architecture is a cultural production; it articulates cultural values spatially through the forms and organizations of buildings, technically through the choice of materials and means of construction, and discursively through the construction of the canon by the critical establishment. What, in this light, can architectural autonomy mean? At first sight, the claims for architectural autonomy in current criticism seems oddly anachronistic, a latter-day *art pour l'art*. I would like to examine the implication of the claims to autonomy in current criticism and show that autonomy is itself an effect of certain modes of criticism.

Autonomy may be understood as self-sufficiency: architecture as self-evident, immediately accessible, open to our cognition and appreciation. Note that in this case architecture is understood as the actual structure and that reception is presumed to be earnest, direct, and uninformed. Oddly enough, this belief in the transparency of architecture is a common assumption of both modernist and postmodernist claims. In modernist dogma it serves to legitimate a spartan sensibility by advocating the use of geometric shapes and primary colors as a universal language.[32] In postmodernism, it legitimates a hedonistic sensibility by invoking easily recognizable themes, popular cliches, even naturalistic forms and anthropomorphic shapes—as if their use could guarantee direct communication.

This view of buildings as isolated objects is quite peculiar. It is as if buildings came into the world through immaculate conception, or, more appropriately for a secular world, appeared like Athena in the head of the architect, the father Zeus, through godlike genius. The critic, by emphasizing the role of the architect as singular author, acquires by association the authority to speak.

The desire for a total transparency of reception is epistemologically naive; it presumes an untenable empiricism. It fails to recognize that our knowledge of the world is always culturally mediated, and therefore fails to see how criticism frames architecture. In other words, it fails to see how the autonomy of the architectural object is an effect of its presence in the virtual space created by criticism. By ignoring the roles of critical discourse and human agency in the construction of architecture—assuming the building as a given— the building is fetishized.

Autonomy may also be understood as self-referential and architecture as intertextual, with buildings referring to other buildings. Architecture in this case refers to both buildings and canon; this view implies that reception is mediated through the schemata and expectations established by the tradition and built into the actual structures. This allows for a more complex understanding of reception as potentially ironical or satirical. While this is undoubtedly a more sophisticated claim for autonomy, its hermetic character is highly problematic, as well as its association with an extreme aestheticism. This position is also politically suspect; it asserts the autonomy of architecture as an art to counter the modernist faith in architecture as a socially and politically engaged praxis. From this perspective we may question the anachronistic appearance of this art-for-art's-sake posture in current architectural debates.

Autonomy may also be understood as self-governance. This is a political claim, implying that the criteria for judging architectural production are established within the architectural community; in other words, that the producers are in the position to establish their own rules (here, again, architecture is an inclusive term, referring to the building, the canon, and the practice of the discipline.)

To recognize the political dimension of architectural judgment is to acknowledge that reception is culturally mediated, through both cognitive schemata and socially established norms of propriety and *bienséance*—in other words, that aesthetic judgment as a problem of taste and sensibility is culturally and historically situated.[33] From this perspective, architecture is a social construct. Following Peter Burger, the autonomy of architecture as an art is a form of mediation of art and society. It is an effect of a particular social figuration, namely modern liberal bourgeois culture, that allows a social space for art to exercise its claims of autonomy. (This stands in vivid contrast to the situation in the Soviet Union or in China during the Cultural Revolution, where autonomous cultural critique was simply impossible.) In this sense autonomy is not an ontological condition of buildings. Rather, it is an effect of criticism as a mode of self-governance. It asserts the freedom to judge architecture on cultural and intellectual terms that transcend the exigencies of day-to-day professional practice. Through the practice of criticism, the highest criteria of excellence are adjudicated by peers and not simply by clients; success in this arena confers prestige and status rather than financial gain.

Autonomy in this sense does have a political value; it allows for the critical articulation of broader values contesting the profit motive and end-means rationality as the only modes of reason. Autonomy is not a given but results from a contestable practice as a challenge to the common-sense pragmatism of the profession and the culture it represents.[34]

Is this type of self-governance really possible in the context of *Real-Politik* of real-estate competition? Is it desirable in a democratic society to set up an elite of cognoscenti with the exclusive ability to determine architectural value? By narrowing the circle of participants, could it condemn to marginality precisely those values for which it wants to stand? While the belief in architecture as an autonomous art has had a heuristic value in challenging the status quo, at this historical juncture it is not self-critical enough. Rather than provide an enlightened perspective, its *promesse de bonheur* conceals the actual relations of power at work, and therefore contributes to false consciousness. For this reason, an adequate critical stance needs to address the conditions of architectural production and the modes of architectural criticism.

CRITIQUE OF CRITICISM

To engage in a critique of architectural criticism is daunting; it presents an aporia: theoretical reflection on criticism, or metacriticism, is itself critique. Furthermore, any account of criticism needs to address how the structure of criticism has changed historically while recognizing its own historicity.[35] Compounding the difficulties is the problematic relationship between criticism and its architectural object. First, there is the question of hierarchy, since criticism as commentary is a supplement to its object yet constitutes it at the level of the canon. Second, there is the problem of translation, since criticism is primarily a discursive and architecture a non-discursive practice.

At this historical juncture significant architectural critique has a difficult if not impossible task: it has to be self-reflective—able to recognize the aporias, the built-in structural contradictions; it ought to be critical of its own presuppositions and address the distinctive features of architecture in terms of its production, social context, and cultural significance while avoiding a simplistic determinism. It needs to address how architecture is autonomous not in essence but as a result of distinctive framing operations provided by criticism. To say this is to be prescriptive and to posit criteria for what constitutes a valid architectural critique: I have in fact ignored my own injunctions against an a priori prescription for criticism.

These tribulations form an ellipse; criticism is a retracing of an orbit that is incomplete, since it never comes full circle. Hence these elliptical remarks, incomplete and yet enacting through their trajectory the various modes of criticism. The form of this essay is an ellipse, starting with criticism as the producer of the architectural canon, followed by criticism as discourse and as judgment, and concluding with a critique of the critical claim that architecture is an autonomous realm. The trajectory of this essay incorporates its subject; it includes commentary, criticism, and critique. The aim has been to disclose the conditions that enable criticism—including this essay—to take place as a cultural practice.

This presents a quandary. It implicitly establishes a hierarchy of various modes of criticism, the lowest being commentary and the highest self-critical critique. This valuation can be justified if one assumes critical self-reflection is in and of itself valuable. This assumption, however, is ultimately an act of faith in the ultimate value of disclosure, of unmasking false claims; it affirms Enlightenment values. Such a relentless engagement in self-criticism, in the pursuit of the "hermeneutics of suspicion" might result in nihilism and cynicism, paralyzing our ability to act, to build the world, both literally and metaphorically.[36] Perhaps the pursuit of critique is profoundly antithetical to the interests of architecture; this is a danger that needs to be acknowledged. Nevertheless, this danger is only present in a condition of alienation in which one assumes that criticism is an autonomous institution. Since criticism, like architecture, is both a set of practices and an institution, it is always situated within a historical frame.[37] This historical frame provides criticism with specificity. Criticism is always a reflection on something, whether historical or contemporary, whether an artifact or a theory. The object of criticism, however, is not simply given. It is reconstructed through discourse. Criticism is not parasitical; it is a productive activity—constructing its object, creating the canon, and implicitly and explicitly defining the criteria for judgment.

Criticism can retrieve, reopen, reformulate, and resituate even the most canonical object.[38] When most productive, it provides new insights and enlivens even the most jaded sensibilities. Recently, architectural criticism has become more open-ended by encouraging the ongoing reinterpretation of the canon, more inclusive in its willingness to admit a greater variety and number of buildings as well as texts and drawings to the canon, and more pluralistic through an increased range of sites, agents, and conventions. With these developments, the critique of criticism has become more self-reflective and its task more problematic due to both the expansion of the space of critical discourse and the complexity of its multiple intersecting trajectories—trajectories that do not return us to a point of origin but lead us to new questions, new possibilities, and new challenges.

1. This distinction is analogous to that between literature and fiction.
2. "Paradox is a kind of semantic confusion, where the two terms in supposed contradiction are not really commensurable." John Guillory, "The Ideology of Cannon Formation: T. S. Eliot and Cleanth Brooks," *Critical Inquiry* 10, no.1 (September 1983): 189.
3. Joseph Kerman, "A Few Canonic Variations," *Critical Inquiry* 10, no.1 (September 1983): 107.
4. Guillory, "Canon Formation."
5. Bannister Fletcher, *A History of Architecture* 18th ed. (New York: Scribners, 1975).
6. The texts establishing the canon of modern architecture include: Walter Gropius, *Internationale Architektur* (1925); Ludwig Hilberseimer, *Internationale neue Baukunst* (Stuttgart, 1926); G.A. Platz, *Die Baukunst der neuesten Zeit* (Berlin, 1927); P. Meyer, *Modern Architektur und Tradition* (Zurich, 1928); H. R. Hitchcock, *Modern Architecture, Romanticism and Reintegration* (New York, 1929), Bruno Taut, *Die neue Baukunst in Europa und Amerika* (Stuttgart, 1929); M.Malkiel-Jirmounsky, *Les tendances de l'architecture contemporaine* (Paris, 1930); S. Cheney, *The New World Architecture* (London, 1930); Fillia, *La nuova architettura* (Turin, 1931); A. Sartoris, *Gli elementi dell'architettura razionale* (Milan, 1932). Notable recent works include: Kenneth Frampton, *Modern Architecture, A Critical History* (New York, 1980) and William Curtis, *Modern Architecture since 1900* (Oxford, 1982).
7. In fact, the Chrysler and Empire State Buildings were included in the modern canon in the 1970s when Art Deco was rehabilitated as a serious style. The criteria for inclusion in the canon remained mainly stylistic, with minimal attention to other architectural considerations such as monumentality, urbanistic impact, innovative technology or program, and popular iconography.
8. For Kant, aesthetic judgment is "disinterested," and disinterest is achieved by holding in abeyance one's judgment on social dimensions. His choice of a palace is perfect, because architecture more than any other art points to the tension between political and aesthetic judgement. Kant still acknowledges the social and political dimensions, which later aesthetic critics would efface. See: Immanuel Kant, *Critique of Judgment*, trans. J. H. Bernard (New York: Hafner Press, MacMillan, 1951), 38. Also quoted in Peter Burger, *Theory of the Avant Garde* (Minneapolis: University of Minnesota Press, 1984), 43.
9. For a discussion of the normative roles of paradigms in science see Thomas Kuhn, *The Structure of Scientific Revolutions*, 2nd ed., Foundations of the Unity of Science Series, vol.2, no.2 (Chicago: University of Chicago Press, 1970).
10. Vitruvius, *The Ten Books On Architecture*, trans. Morris H. Morgan (New York: Dover,1960).
11. The *Cambridge Camden Society* was founded in 1839 and established *The Eclesiologist* in 1841. Quoted in Peter Collins, *Changing Ideals in Modern Architecture* (London: Faber and Faber, 1965), 109.
12. On the relation of transgression to decorum, see Miriam Gusevich, "Decoration and Decorum: Adolf Loos' Critique of Kitsch," *New German Critique*, 43 (1988): 97-124 and Miriam Gusevich, "Purity and Transgression: Reflections on the Architectural Avant-garde's Rejection of Kitsch," *Discourse*, X.1 (fall-winter 1988): 90-115.
13. On the historicity of aesthetic categories see Peter Burger, *Theory of the Avant-Garde* (Minneapolis: University of Minnesota Press, 1984), 15-16.
14. This is clearly exemplified by *The Harvard Architectural Journal*, the *Princeton Architectural Journal*, the *Cornell Architectural Journal*, *VIA* (University of Pennsylvania), *Precis* (Columbia University), etc. *Oppositions*, the distinguished organ of the Institute for Architecture and Urban Studies in New York throughout the 1970s, was not affiliated with a larger academic institution and was discontinued when the institute closed; its intellectual heir, *Assemblage*, has firmer academic connections and will hopefully survive longer.

15. In this class, prestige is assigned to design-oriented journals (*Architectural Record, Progressive Architecture*, etc.) over the more exclusively business and construction journals such as *Construction News*.
16. Magazines for mass circulation range from fashionable journals like *HG* and *Metropolitan Home*, to how-to magazines like *Popular Mechanics*.
17. For a discussion of economic, social, and cultural capital in the constitution of taste see Pierre Bourdieu, *Distinction: A Social Critique of the Judgement of Taste*, trans. Richard Nice (Cambridge: Harvard University Press, 1984). The contest between cultural and economic capital accounts for the ongoing critiques of dominant economic institutions by architectural critics representing architecture as a cultural institution; it is part of the animosity between intellectuals and businessmen. It is noteworthy that active professionals are situated in the middle, bridging the gap between culture and money and the values and aesthetic preferences of these two subcultures.
18. Architectural criticism, unlike literary criticism, is still remarkably prudish; sexuality is still a taboo, as are gender, race, religion, and class. For instance, Erich Mendelsohn is one of the first significant Jewish architects the majority of whose commissions came from Jewish patrons in Germany, Israel, and the United States, yet this significant background information is rarely acknowledged or critically incorporated in assessments of Mendelsohn's work. Similarly, the historical force of an "old boys network" in the architectural profession and the extent to which homosexuality has provided a particular kind of male bonding that informed aesthetic preferences remains a secret text of architecture, with more mysteries to be revealed than those at the Masonic Lodges. A significant exception is the remarkable book by Rudolf and Margot Wittkower, *Born Under Saturn: the character and conduct of artists* (New York: W.W. Norton and Company, 1963).
19. For an intelligent discussion of this issue see John Whiteman, "Architectural Representation in the Age of Criticism," *The Harvard Architectural Review* 6 (Cambridge: MIT Press), 136-47.
20. Criticism, from the greek *krinein* means "to separate, to cut into," and "to judge, to discern." It is also related to a discerning decision, a decisive point, a crisis (*kriosis*). I would like to deploy these various senses to elucidate the problematic relation of architecture and criticism. Walter W. Skeat, *An Etymological Dictionary of the English Language*, 4th ed. (Oxford: Oxford University Press,1974).
21. Still, we must recognize the constraints under which many architectural critics operate. If they are free-lancing they do not have the protection of a permanent position and they need to rely on the goodwill of the editor of the journal as well as the architect whose work is being reviewed. Under these conditions one must be very courageous or very foolhardy to criticize established architects, for one risks offending people and being excommunicated. These are some of the reasons why "serious" criticism is most often encountered within the halls of academia. It is the privilege of the academic who has a relatively secure position
22. Friedreich Nietzsche, *The Use and Abuse of History*, trans. Adrian Collins (Indianapolis: Bobbs Merrill Co., 1957), 8.
23. Colin Rowe and Fred Koetter, *Collage City* (Cambridge: MIT Press, 1975), Manfredo Tafuri, *Theories and History of Architecture*, trans. Giorgio Verrecha (New York: Harper and Row, 1980); Manfredo Tafuri, *The Sphere and the Labyrinth: Avant Gardes and Architecture from Piranesi to the 1970s*, trans. Pellegrino d'Acierno and Robert Connelly (Cambridge: MIT Press, 1987).
24. On the loss of faith question see Rowe and Koetter, *Collage City* and "Beyond the Modern Movement," *The Harvard Architectural Review*, vol. 1, (Cambridge: MIT Press, 1980); on positivism in architecture critically viewed see Robert Venturi and Denise Scott Brown, *Learning from Las Vegas* (Cambridge: MIT Press, 1977).
25. Theodore Adorno, *The Jargon of Authenticity*, trans. Knut Tarnowski and Frederic Will (Evanston: Northwestern University Press, 1973).

GUSEVICH

26. *Deconstruction in Architecture: An Architectural Design Profile*. (London: Academy Editions, New York: St. Martin's Press, 1988).
27. For an intelligent discussion of the critical relation of architecture and philosophy see: Andrew Benjamin, "Derrida, Architecture and Philosophy," *Deconstruction in Architecture*, 8-11.
28. Jacques Derrida, "White Mythology," trans. F.C.T. Moore *New Literary History* 6 (1974). 1: 89-106. Originally published as "La mythologie blanche" in *Rhetorique et Philosophie, Poetique* 5 (Paris: Editions du Seuil, 1971)
29. Paul Ricoeur, *The Rule of Metaphor: Multidisciplinary Studies of the Creation of Meaning in Language* (Toronto: University of Toronto Press, 1977), 7, 248, 254.
30. Of the extensive literature on type, I here point specifically to the writings of Giulio Argan, Carlo Aymonino, Giorgio Grassi, Aldo Rossi, Massimo Scolari, Oriol Bohigas, Alan Colquhoun, and Anthony Vidler. Most of these authors refer to Quatremere de Quincy's neoclassical definition of type in *Dictionnaire Historique d'Architecture*.
31. For a comprehensive set of writings on the autonomy of architecture see *Autonomous Architecture*, vol. 3 of *The Harvard Architectural Review*, (Cambridge: MIT Press, 1984).
32. Reyner Banham, *Theory and Design in the First Machine Age* (Cambridge: MIT Press, 1980).
33. On the importance of decorum to architecture see: Norbert Elias, *The Court Society (Die Hofische Gesselschaft)*, trans. Edmund Jephcott (Oxford: Blackwell, 1983), ch. 3; and Miriam Gusevich, "Decoration and Decorum, Adolf Loos' Critique of Kitsch," *New German Critique*, no. 43 (1988): 97-124.
34. This is exemplified by the critical writings of both Augustus W. N. Pugin and John Ruskin.
35. Dominick La Capra, "Writing the History of Criticism Now?" *History and Criticism* (Ithaca: Cornell University Press, 1985), 95-114.
36. Paul Ricouer, *Freud and Philosophy: An essay on Interpretation*, trans. Denis Savage (New Haven: Yale University Press, 1970), 32-36.
37. La Capra, *History and Criticism*, 95-114.
38. On the productive capacities of criticism see: T.S. Elliot, "Tradition and Individual Talent," *Selected Essays* (London: Faber and Faber, 1932); Umberto Eco, *The Open Work*, trans. Anna Cancogni (Cambridge: Harvard University Press, 1989), 1-23, 85-104.

PEGGY DEAMER

SUBJECT, OBJECT, TEXT

Thence follows a consequence of capital importance: it is that external perception is a true hallucination . . . therefore, when we walk in the street, watching and listening to what passes around us, we have within us the various phantoms which would be experienced by a sufferer from hallucinations, shut up in his room and in whose case the visual, auditory, and tactile sensations which are produced in our case by the action of the nerves would all be produced in the same order but without the medium of the nerves. These various "phantoms" are in our case, as in his, houses, roads, carriages, pavements, and passers-by. Only, in our case, there are objects and external events, independent of ourselves and real . . . which correspond to our phantoms.[1]—Hippolyte Taine

Vision as hallucination. Structures, architecture, cityscapes that are no more real than, well, visions. Or rather, visions that are as real as that to which they correspond. Taine's description of seeing is doubly damned: it has neither the authority of mimetic accuracy, nor the freedom of hallucination, shackled as it is by its *Dopplegang*—the exterior world. It is as if vision has been displaced from the world we normally believe it to inhabit but not provided a new locus. The space of this displacement, which Taine so accurately identifies, is the ambiguous territory explored by certain critics—those who simultaneously put there faith in vision and recognize that what they describe is not the object but the mirage behind the ocular plane. It is, as Roland Barthes described Georges Bataille's perceptual sensibility, vision as the avatar of the imagination.[2]

Anyone sufficiently enlightened to contemplate the essence of art will discover many new beauties by comparing the structure of Greek figures with that of modern works, especially when they follow nature rather than the old style. In most modern statues, one finds many small and altogether too minute wrinkles in places where the skin is pinched. On the other hand, the analogous parts of Greek statues shows these wrinkles merging into each other in gentle, wavy curves that unify the whole area. The skin of these masterpieces shows no strains but only gentle tension: it is supported by healthy flesh without bulges. Thus it follows even the fullest contours with perfect smoothness and never produces those particular, willful little wrinkles that we observe on our bodies. Similarly, modern works display too many and too sensuous dimples, while in ancient statuary dimples are used with subtlety and wisdom, reflecting the physical perfection of the Greeks. Often only the trained eye can discover them.[3]—Johann J. Winckelmann

Winckelmann indulged his eye. Indeed, his contribution to art history rests precisely on this: Instead of turning to the artist's biography or historical events to evaluate and differentiate styles, he relied on his perception of the object. He thereby instigated a new chapter in art writing by introducing aesthetics into the critical framework. Embedded in his approach is the prototype of modern art texts: historical essays that develop "stories" about art's development; critical writings that evaluate either the aesthetic worth or cultural value of an object or trend; and theoretical writings that reevaluate the meaning of aesthetics, its social status, and its cultural values.

But clearly there is something else going on in the above quote that this deserved claim to fame overlooks. Has not Winckelmann come too close to the object? While his vision is accurate—and we see more in the statue than we would otherwise—it is hardly the account of a neutral observer. His concern for the wrinkles, bulges, and dimples is slightly unseemly. Indeed, there is an underlying tension between the concentration that he lavishes on the object— bracketed off, as it is, from other qualifying criteria—and the contextualization that lies at the heart of the traditional art writing with which Winckelmann is associated. Unlike history, theory, or criticism as we know it, the writing demonstrated here is based on a vision too bound to its object to allow for diachronic or synchronic comparisons, analytic or prescriptive generalizations. It explores, instead, that space between the object and its absorption by the viewer.

[B]eginning and ending are determinations implicit in the very nature of a column as a support and on this account must come into appearance on it as constituent features of its own. This is the reason why developed and beautiful architecture supplies the column with a pedestal and a capital. It is true that in the Tuscan Order there is no pedestal so that the column rises directly from the ground; but in that case its length is something fortuitous for the eye; we do not know whether the column has been pressed so and so deeply into the ground by the weight of the mass supported. If the beginning of the column is not to seem vague and accidental, it must be given on purpose a foot on which it stands and which expressly reveals the beginning as a beginning. By this means art intends, for one thing, to bring to the notice of our eye the solidity and safety of the structure and, as it were, set our eye at rest in this respect. For the like reason art makes the column end with a capital which indicates the column's real purpose of load-bearing and also means: 'Here the column ends.' This reflection on the intentionally made beginning and end provides the really deeper reason for having a pedestal and a capital... Organic products, as they are portrayed by sculpture in the shape of animals and men, have their beginning and end in their own free outlines, because it is the rational organism itself which settles the boundaries of its shape from within outward. For the column and its shape, however, architecture has nothing but the mechanical determinant of load-bearing and the spatial distance from the ground to the point where the load to be carried terminates the column. But the particular aspects implicit in this determinant belong to the column, and art must bring them out and give shape to them.[4]—G. W. F. Hegel

Hegel's analysis of the column is not what is expected from the principal formulator of idealism, the philosopher of a painstaking chronology of the Spirit's realization, the writer whose work is one of the primary examples of and apologias for romanticism. What surprises is not merely the subject matter—the mundane column— but the writing's concreteness and particularity. Idealism is couched in empiricism, in a visuality at odds with the message we know it ultimately contains. One suspects that this message and the reputed idealism, like those of Winckelmann, have prevented readers from focusing on the particularity of the way Hegel sees and thinks.

It is important to realize that Hegel's Spirit-culminating system (which in the *Aesthetics* goes from the most concrete to the most ephemeral, from architecture to poetry and philosophy) is not based on a denial of the concrete but on concreteness's own dialectic transformation. Hegel's "reading" of the object is achieved not through generalization or abstraction but through attention to the universal embedded in the particular. Hegel's "things are what they are only by virtue of the divine and thereby creative thought that dwells within them" resembles Ezra Pound's more radically phrased Imagist dictum, "Don't use such an expression as 'dim lights of peace.' It dulls the image. It mixes an abstraction with the concrete. It comes from the writer's not realizing that the natural object is always the adequate symbol!"[5] At the same time, however, the specificity of this "vision" is *not* based on "fact." Hegel, like Winckelmann, is not describing the object but his response to it. It is the empirical domain drawn into the imagination. But where Winckelmann responded to the surface particulars of the statue, Hegel projects an inner vitality onto the column, an inner life given in the act of its viewing.

Hegel's idealism, wherein the Spirit comes to self-realization through man's self-realization, and man's self-realization comes through the works and objects he posits around him, is essentially a philosophy of Russian- doll-like identifications between successive subjects and objects. It is one in which the final object, architecture (despite its ultimate inertness) is in the odd position of having to absorb the thrust of the subjective projections directed its way. The column is at once assumed to be like a person—hence its susceptibility to weight and pressure, its need for a foot, its urge toward speech, the self-reflexive search for identity—and distinct from the human body, as if its natural "objectness" was not enough to establish this fact. It is a type of empathetic projection that avoids the pitfalls of anthropocentrism even as it fails to distinguish the object's autonomy from the subject. If Hegel's vision of the column isn't as robustly physical as Winckelmann's of the male statue, it nevertheless gives equal evidence that the body is implicit in vision.

Classical architecture also knew the projection, and used it on occasions... The corner projections of the Cancelleria are piers which we can also imagine separated from the main surface... The projection has its roots in the surface, from which it cannot be separated without vital injury to the body. In this way the projecting central portion of the Palazzo Barberini is to be understood, and, still more typical, because less noticeable, the famous pilaster facade of the Palazzo Odescalchi in Rome which advances slightly in front of the unarticulated wings... the treatment of the main body and wings is of such a kind that the impression of the plane running through the whole remains quite subordinate to the dominant recessional motive. In the same way, even the modest dwelling house was able to deprive the wall of its sheer plane character by quite trivial projections, until, about 1800, a new generation arises which pays full tribute to the plane.[6]—Heinrich Wölfflin

Wölfflin is subtle with his self-projection: there is really only the "injury to the body," the personification of the dwelling-house, that deprives the wall of its character. Yet his position vis-à-vis the object disturbs our understanding of what constitutes vision and visual analysis. Projections and planes—formal conditions that lack any actual objectness—are treated not only as if embodied but as if they were dignitaries; one century knows them, another pays tribute to them. If Hegel's column was reinvented as an object capable of containing human attributes, Wölfflin personifies these attributes and invents the object to which they will conform. He is clearly looking hard at the building; it is just that what he sees is not on the far side of his retina. It is a form of hallucination.[7]

To a certain extent this condition is consistent with Wölfflin's empathy with the object, similar to Hegel's but rooted more strictly in neo-Kantian theory. Following Theodor Lipps, who located empathetic response between the enjoyment of "sensuous objects distinct from myself" and "the enjoyment of myself" in the realm of "objectivated self-enjoyment . . . (in which I) find, or feel myself,"[8] Wölfflin made clear that he understood the object's character as a literal projection of his physical self. "We judge every object by analogy with our bodies. The object . . . will not only transform itself immediately into a creature, with head and foot, back and front; and not only are we convinced that this creature must feel ill at ease if it does not stand upright and seems about to fall over, but we go so far as to experience, to a highly sensitive degree, the spiritual condition and contentment or discontent expressed by any configuration, however different from ourselves."[9] And while Wölfflin's texts also demonstrate how deeply empathy is embedded in language—the use of terms like "body" or "wing" when referring to a building is not, strictly speaking, fantastic—writers of this genre indicate that such conventions are not to be taken lightly, that the manipulated vocabulary is neither incidental nor innocent.

Such writers also reveal how thoroughly this grammar is intertwined with that of formalism; the personification implicit in empathy provides the essential structure of formalism's language. Not only are formal conditions reinvented as characters, but, as Wölfflin's texts most amply demonstrate, abstract phenomena such as "classical architecture" or "art" are seen as willful personalities that direct the course of history. While we tend to associate formalism with a reductive investigation of the compositional "facts" of the object, we forget that it depends on a wild leap of the imagination that invents abstract entities from perceived configurations. Such invention says as much about the perceiving subject as the perceived object and makes the formalist's story more enticing than the author might acknowledge.[10]

[A] marble surface receives in its age hues of continually increasing glow and grandeur; . . . its undecomposing surface preserves a soft, fruit-like polish forever, slowly flushed by the maturing sun of centuries. Hence, while in the Northern Gothic the effort of the architect was always so to diffuse his ornament as to prevent the eye from permanently resting on the blank material, the Italian fearlessly left fallow large fields of uncarved surface, and concentrated the labour of the chisel on detached portions, in which the eye, being rather directed to them by their isolation than attracted by their salience, required perfect finish and pure design rather than force of space or breadth of parts.[11]—John Ruskin

Ruskin's writing is more overtly about the object itself than the idea for which the object provides example, and herein lies its affinity with description. In *The Art of Describing* Svetlana Alpers distinguishes between the "narrative" tradition of the Italian Renaissance and the "descriptive" tradition of Dutch seventeenth-century painting. Relating the Dutch artists to the empiricism of Bacon and Locke and their eschewal of representation based on hierarchy, proportion, and mathematics for one dwelling on the surface as fact,[12] Alpers gives an account of description that in many ways accords with the intrinsically surface-bound, two-dimensional criticism demonstrated above. But Ruskin's writing (perhaps more clearly than that of the others) resists the implication that this attention to surface precludes associative references. Ruskin's eyes seek to possess the desired object in order to unlock the secret power that the surface holds. Nor did this concern for the two-dimensional stem merely from an attraction to the object's sensual surface; for Ruskin, the two-dimensionality of vision was an epistemological position. A true inheritor of the Lockian tradition, which held that we see in two dimensions and interpret the third only through the imposition of touch memory, Ruskin wanted to recapture the flat imagery of childhood. Once abstracted to two dimensions at the moment of viewing, the image was for him inherently open to symbolism. As Ruskin put it, "You do not see with the lens of the eye. You see through it, and by means of that, but you see with the soul of the eye."[13]

Despite Ruskin's Victorian moralism (and unconsummated marriage), this soul was not divorced from his body, and his "descriptions" invoked a spectrum of physical desire. While he speaks of the marble as if it were a fruit, he responds to it as a man caressing a woman; here Ruskin's own sensuality surfaces.[14] Unlike description, criticism of this kind—evocative criticism—is not, then, a literary surrogate for the visually absent object; the object is created anew by evoking physical sensations that form its epistemological structure.

He who thus penetrated into the most secret parts of nature preferred always the more to the less remote, what, seemingly exceptional, was an instance of law more refined, the construction about things of a peculiar atmosphere and mixed lights . . . In him first appears the taste for what is bizarre and recherche in landscape; . . . all the solemn effects of moving water . . . springing from its distant source among the rocks on the heath of the Madonna of the Balconies, passing, as a little fall, in the treacherous calm of the Madonna of the Lake, next as a goodly river, below the Madonna of the Rocks, washing the white walls of its distant villages, stealing out in a network of divided streams in La Gioconda to the seashore of the St. Anne–that delicate place where the wind passes like the hand of some finer ether over the surface . . . and the tops of the rocks, to which the waves never rise, are green with grass, grown fine as hair . . . Through Leonardo's strange veil of sight things reach him so; in no ordinary night or day, but as in faint light of eclipse, or in some brief interval of falling rain at day break, or through deep water.[15]—Walter Pater

Pater, confirming a longstanding rivalry with Ruskin about his visual acuity, is reported to have insisted, "I cannot believe that Ruskin saw more in the church at St. Mark than I do!"[16] But despite this plea for empirical mastery, Pater had ultimate faith in subjective indulgence. As he put it, "the first condition of [criticism] . . . must be, of course, to know yourself, to have ascertained your own senses exactly."[17] In the end Pater was more guilty than his predecessor of what Proust had called "idolatry," the lust for the object beyond the bounds of objectivity. Where Ruskin's idolatry was tempered by thought that, in Proust's terms, "has incarnated itself in the bodies of sculpted marble [and] snowy mountains," Pater's remained unbound by the external data.

Thus, while a dialectic struggle between subject and object occurs, for Ruskin, Wölfflin, and Winckelmann, on the plane of the retina, Pater's objects cannot survive the thrust of his subjective gaze. They are subsumed and wholly reconstituted by it. In the above passage, the composite da Vincian landscape on which he breathily lavishes so much attention is an illusion. We are reminded that Pater was an avid reader of Taine and understood that vision was coplanar with hallucination.

But if the object's "factuality" is dissolved by Pater's gaze, his own personality takes on a surprising presence in his texts. Just as the subjects of Pater's "Imaginary Portraits" are variations on his personality, Leonardo in the above quoted essay is a vessel for Pater's ideal self. As "author" he also draws particular attention to the role of writing in the mutual definition of subject and object, whose simultaneous disintegration leaves a void filled by language, by the literariness of the prose that Pater puts in their place. Like the poetry of Coleridge, Wordsworth, and Blake—to whom Pater's attention to visual stimulation can be compared—this writing is not really about the image as much as the literary tropes used to create it. At the same time, its self-consciousness reveals the extent to which Pater becomes "other" in his role as author; how much the self, to quote Barthes, "apprehends itself *elsewhere*" and finds itself unanchored, shifted, taken apart.[18]

The building, which provokes by its beauty a positive response, resuscitates an early hunger or greed in the disposition of morsels that are smooth with morsels that are rough, or of wall-space with the apertures; an impression, I have said, composed as well from other architectural sensations. To repeat: it is as if those apertures had been torn in that body by our revengeful teeth so that we experience as a beautiful form, and indeed as indispensable shelter also, the outcome of sadistic attacks, fierce yet smoothed, healed into a source of health which we would take inside us and preserve there unharmed for the source of our goodness: as if also—the apposition though contradictory should cause no surprise—as if the smooth body of the wall-face, or the smooth vacancy within the apertures, were the shining breast, while the mouldings, the projections, the rustications, the tiles, were the head, the feeding nipple of that breast.[19]—Adrian Stokes

In an early text Stokes describes the manner in which a male sculptor shaping his material with a chisel as if making love to a woman produces their (male) children in statuary.[20] In his later writing, of which the above is an example, this literal metaphor of the object's making gives way to a more subtle and phenomenological means of looking: the sexuality between subject and object is part of the interpretive eye, not merely of the hand. Yet it is not the sexuality felt by the lover for his mistress; Stokes clung to the visible object the way a child clings to its mother—object, like mother, being proof of an "other" from which one is different but upon which one depends.

Stokes, following Ruskin, considered sight the paradigm of senses because it alone was direct, "innocent," unaffected by knowledge. But he went further than Ruskin in describing this dominance in terms of physical ascendancy. Stokes believed that the inner structure of the eye appears in visual perception (a physical counterpart to Ruskin's "you see with the soul of the eye"), and that the whole of the body through all its senses—especially touch—was absorbed in the act of seeing. And because this body was necessarily a sexual— indeed, Oedipal—body, Stokes's reaction to the external world was always highly charged.

Reading Stokes, then, can never be neutral. Winckelmann disguised his own lust by absorbing it into the physicality of the statue he described; Ruskin merely ignored the fact that a skin's-depth below the surface of the images he described lay the sexual body; Pater sublimated his sexuality, "the flame more eager and devouring," in the general fecundity of his prose. Stokes forces the reader to rub up against the object's image. We must confront the sexuality of the object as boldly as he does.

Stokes's texts also demonstrate the importance of prosody in drawing the reader into this sexual fantasy. His description of the carver making love to his stone could as well portray Stokes's way with words. He admired what Pound called the "carving attitude" toward writing, which regarded words as "consequences of things" as opposed to "the female role, the way of the modeler, that symbolist way with words which regards things, in the last analysis, as the consequence of words that name them."[21] Approaching his textual material accordingly, Stokes manipulated the language to match, in physicality and durability, the objects he praised. Nouns, verbs, and lists constitute a "hard" and immediately present language. And in spite of the tenuous "as if" floating in the above passage, he avoids both the metaphors that make the tropes self-conscious and the adjectives that make the "poetry" of associations apparent. Stokes does not convey the impression that a building is like a mother; he assumes it *is* a mother.

Sensorially evocative criticism relies on a certain epistemological position vis-à-vis the object, a position dependent at once on the almost physical mental space linking subject and object and the extreme abstraction engendered when the tightness of that space results in a certain myopia. This stance, an inversion of the neoclassical subordination of part to whole, decontextualizes the object physically and mentally. Despite the original condemnation of Taine's doubly damned vision, the image is both freed from preconceived notions and granted authority via monumentalization. It is seen as a thing-in-itself.

Nevertheless, the object is ultimately denied this seeming autonomy. It is instead absorbed into perhaps the most profound of contexts—the self. The eye, the pivotal mechanism in this recontextualization, is obsessed with accuracy just as it spurns the empiricism generally associated with visual acuity. Likewise, the gaze sights a line that approaches both "the tyranny of the eye" associated with modernism and formalism and the sexual indulgence associated with Freud and Bataille. Evocative writers have contributed significantly to the literature of formalism just as they have broken its bounds with the physicality of their visual response. Indeed, evocative criticism indicates that these supposedly divergent aspects of criticism—formalism and psycho-phenomenal "deconstructions"— are perhaps opposite sides of the same coin. Given the fantastic aspects of formalism's disengagement from reality and deconstructivism's continued fascination with the power of the eye (even as it attempts to disturb its authority), the opposition between these two viewpoints is obscured.

If evocative criticism is defined in part by this epistemological position—the visual elision of subject and object, observer and observed—it is equally defined by its literary position—verbal elision between writer and reader. Its writers demonstrate how seriously the language of the critical text is to be taken, how much the prose must inhere in the reader at the same time it adheres to the object. The object must not merely be recreated *for* the reader but conceived *by* the reader; the image offered us must become our own.

This kind of writing draws on the classical style of *ekphrasis*, which, according to Hermogenes, "must contrive to bring about seeing through hearing."[22] It plays havoc with Lessing's dictum that the arts be kept distinct because each appeals to different sensibilities; such prose does not strive for the logic of sequential linearity associated with narrative but, again in the words of Hermogenes, for the "clarity and visibility" associated with the visual arts.[23] Indeed, there is an implicit assumption that the mental image is equal parts of sight and word, vision and story. But this prose differs from *ekphrasis* in a significant manner, for Hermogenes specifies that the mode of expression, the style, should fit the subject matter: "[I]f the subject is florid, let the style be florid, too, and if the subject be dry, let the style be the same." Evocative criticism, instead, does not attend to the exterior object (the subject matter) but to the subjectively manufactured, the literarily troped image. Thus Stokes, with his carving fixation, reminds us of Theophile Gautier, who pointed out that the original meaning of "epigram" is writing incised upon a slab;[24] while Pater, believing that all art (including writing) strove to be like music, wrote prose that was soft and flaccid, that did not land on its object, but floated above it.

It is interesting to compare this evocative criticism with more recent "deconstructivist" texts. Not only do the latter provide most poignant elucidations of the "evocative" texts,[25] they share an interest in the collapse of inner and outer worlds. But the circumstances informing each approach are ultimately so distinct as to render a comparison specious. Evocative criticism resists attempts by connoisseurs and aestheticians to defer to chronology, biography, and popular taste and attends primarily to the object. Poststructuralist criticism, on the other hand, is a reaction to the faith in empirical fact and formal evidence that ultimately accompanies such object fixation. There is, in other words, a contextual difference: what the deconstructivists call the over-determination of the object is precisely the recognition that it exists in multiple, indeed unlimited, contexts, all of which threaten its identity. Evocative critics, by contrast, scrutinize the object to the point of its dissolution thus threatening its identity from the other direction. Given their different attitudes toward the object, it is not surprising that while poststructuralist writers appreciate and elucidate evocative texts, they don't in fact, produce them.

Evocative criticism's contribution to critical writing lies, then, in the unique manner in which the object is lodged in the critical process: it is the origin but not the end of the inquiry. While such criticism ultimately describes the story by which the object looses its autonomy under the critic's gaze, it depends initially on a total engagement with the object. Even in its hallucinatory state such criticism precludes the possibility of pure thought or of a critical ideology that sees objects as merely examples of itself. Stokes made his criterion for exemplary art—art that was metaphorically if not actually "carved" (as opposed to modelled)—the artist's willingness to confront the requirements of his material. Likewise, these writers approach their "material" as a resistent, demanding presence. For them, the object is not transparent to something before or behind it, it is not the "representation" of something other than itself. It is the "other" awaiting seduction.

It is the attraction to the object, then, that draws evocative criticism to architecture, whose objects are so, well, objectlike. As a nonrepresentational art, architecture and its buildings provide the objects-as-presence that evocative criticism seeks. Beyond this is the fact that buildings are physical, bodily, and robust. Though empathetic projections are embedded in our general language, architecture draws more than its fair share of such tropes. While we assume that references to buildings that measure physical and psychological well-being are to be taken only half seriously, the ease with which we fall into such language is indicative of architecture's particular corporeality. Evocative criticism, which not only takes this language seriously but plunders its willing subject (matter), massages life into a topic that otherwise has traditionally proved so resistent to critical vitality.

SUBJECT, OBJECT, TEXT

Figure Captions:
Olympia, Temple of Zeus, sculpture of west pediment, from Olympia Museum
Temple of Athena Nike, Athens
Palazzo della Cancelleria, Rome
Santa Maria della Spina, Tuscany, drawing by John Ruskin.
Mona Lisa
San Sebastiano, Venice, photographed by Adrian Stokes

Notes:
1. Hippolyte Taine, *On Intelligence*, trans. T. D. Haye (London: L.Reeve and Co., 1871), 222-24.
2. There is also an interesting discussion regarding the discontinuity between vision and the object in Jonathan Crary's "Modernizing Vision" in *Vision and Visuality*, Hal Foster, ed. (Seattle: Bay Press, 1988), 38-39. Crary describes the work of the German physiologist Johannes Muller who, thirty years before Taine, discovered not only that energy alone can act as a visual stimuli, but that different sources can produce the same visual sensation. While this theory does not describe the radical juncture of fact and image implied by Taine, it nevertheless introduces the idea of the arbitrary relationship between stimulus and sensation.
3. Elizabeth Gilmore Holt, ed. and comp., *A Documentary History of Art*, vol. II, (Princeton: Princeton University Press, 1982), 342-43.
4. T. M. Knox, trans., *Hegel's Aesthetics: Lectures on Fine Art*, vol.II (Oxford: Clarendon Press, 1974), 666-68.
5. Donald Davie, *Ezra Pound* (Chicago: University of Chicago Press, 1975), 32-3.
6. Heinrich Wölfflin, *Principles of Art History* (New York: Dover Publications, 1950), 121-22.
7. For a discussion of Wölfflin's empathetic formalism, see Michael Podro *The Critical Historians of Art* (New Haven: Yale University Press, 1982).
8. Karl Aschenbrenner and Arnold Isenburg, eds., *Aesthetic Theories: Studies in the Philosophy of Art* (Englewood Cliffs, NJ:Prentice Hall, 1965), 403.
9. Heinrich Wölfflin, *Renaissance and Baroque* (Ithaca, NY: Cornell University Press, 1967), 77. Wölfflin studied with Johannes Volkelt at the University of Basel. Volkelt, a neo-Kantian empathetic philosopher, constructed a "metaphysics" of empathy on the absolute noumenal, non-empirical ground of experience, a "trans-subjective subjectivism." He was primarily interested in combatting the idea that our pleasure in looking at objects was based on the English empiricist idea of "association." He felt that empathy was more on an a priori condition than "association" implied.
10. Wölfflin, the quintessential formalist, demonstrates an ambivalence toward this aspect of formalism's episteme. While in his criticism he takes the same stance vis-à-vis the object that he associates with a "Baroque" method of seeing—"[the Baroque] effect presumes that the spectator is able to disregard the merely tangible character of the architectonic form and is capable of surrendering to the visual spectacle, where semblance interweaves with semblance"—he is loath to admit that he actually finds the Baroque more fulfilling than the Classical. (Wölfflin, *Principles*, 69.)
11. Review of Lord Lindsay's "History of Christian Art," par. 20-9, *Works* 12: 107-08.
12. See Martin Jay, "Scopic Regimes of Modernity" in *Vision and Visuality* 13.
13. *Eagles Nest*, par. 98; *Works* 22: 194.
14. Ruskin's language, in his more theoretical moments, attests to this sensuality of vision. He writes:
> There is this strong instinct in me which I cannot analyze to draw and describe things I live—not for reputation, not for the good of others, nor for my own advantage, but a sort of instinct like that for eating and drinking. I should like to draw all St. Mark's, all this Verona stone by stone, to eat it all up into my mind, touch by touch. (Letter to father from Verona, *Works* 10; quoted in the introduction to the volume, xxvi.)

41

He projects this same sensibility onto his loved Venetians:
   Those were the kind of images and shadows they lived on: . . . these thin dry bones of art were nourishing meat to the Venetian race: that they grew and throve on that diet, every day spiritually fatter for it, and more comfortably sound in human soul. (*St. Mark's Rest*, ch. 8, par.110: *Works* 24: 93-4).
And of the imagination Penetrative, he writes:
   a piercing pholas-like mind's tongue, that works and tastes into the very rock heart; . . . all is alike divided asunder, joint and marrow, whatever utmost truth, life principle it has, laid bare . . . (*Modern Painters* II, part 3, sec. 2, ch. 3, par. 3; *Works* 4:251).

15. Walter Pater, *The Renaissance: Studies in Art and Poetry* (Berkeley: University of California Press, 1980), 86-7.

16. Harold Bloom, intro. to *The Selected Writings of Walter Pater*, ed. Harold Bloom, (New York: Columbia University Press, 1974), xvi.

17. Bloom, ibid., 118.

18. Roland Barthes, *Roland Barthes by Roland Barthes*, trans. Richard Howard (New York: Hill and Wang, 1977), 168.

19. Adrian Stokes, *Smooth and Rough*, in *The Critical Writings of Adrian Stokes*, vol. II (London: Thames and Hudson, 1978), 243.

20. The quote is as follows:
   For no other art, not even the Greek, shows so marked a preference for the male nude, a figure far less easily composed to beauty than the female nude. Such unique choice shows a predominance in sculptural fantasy of a feeling for spatial values alone, of a feeling for mass, for material as being the fruitful female block that will give birth to the most active shapes full of prolific sap. And to push this fantasy further, since the architect's building is female, set on the earth like Giorgione's woman by the running stream, the sculptor's attendant statuary are her lovers and sons rather than her daughters or a mere projection of herself. But only sculptors with a passion for the material, stone, will keep so close to this primary fantasy that on their low relief they create for the stone her children in the image of male infants. (118, I).

21. Donald Davie describes these aspects of Pound's work in his *Ezra Pound: Poet as Sculptor* (London: Routledge and Keegan Paul, 1965), 36-39 and 156.

22. This idea of ekphrasis was brought to my attention by Richard Read in his unpublished thesis, *The Evocative Genre of Art Criticism*, (Department of English Literature, University of Reading), 1981.

23. Translated by Michael Baxandall in his *Giotto and the Orators: Humanist Observers of Painting in Italy and the Discovery of Pictorial Composition, 1350-1450* (Oxford: Oxford University Press, 1971), 85.

24. Harold Bloom on Pater and Ruskin; Stephen Bann on Pater and Stokes.

JENNIFER BLOOMER

TOWARDS DESIRING ARCHITECTURE:
PIRANESI'S *COLLEGIO*[1]

PROLOGUE: ON SECTION

A section is an assemblage of dark spots on a plane. It maps the residual of a surgery on an object by a plane of incision. Each spot marks an instant of convergence of an axis of inscription with an axis of incision. The sectioned object undergoes permutations in a logical system of representation—a system of coordinates. The logic of the representation resembles the logic imposed upon the physical world: the logic of gravity. Within this imposed structure, objects are ascribed an orientation with respect to the center of the planet, which becomes translated into an orientation with respect to the surface of the planet. Thus, objects are endowed with tops and bottoms (the parts most distal and most proximal in respective to the planet's center).

On the plane of inscription, the scratchings that represent the object sliced by a plane perpendicular to the line connecting "top" and "bottom" are called "plan." A plan is a section that demands the presence of gravity: "Plan" has concise meaning, therefore, only in

---

1. The following is an expanded version of "Vertex and Vortex: A Tectonics of Section," published previously in *Perspecta* 23 (New York: Rizzoli International, 1987). The Postscript has appeared previously in *Semiotics 87*, the proceedings of the annual meeting of the Semiotics Society of America, where it was titled "'Wicked Architect,' 'Unsafe Building': A Taupology of Piranesi's *Collegio*." Together they constitute Construction Two in Chapter Two of *Desiring Architecture: The Scrypt of Joyce and Piranesi*, forthcoming from the Yale University Press, 1991.

a world where the concepts of "heaviness" and "lightness" are distinct and unambiguous.

We, of course, do not live in such a positivistic paradise. The world and language are tangled around each other. In his astonishingly prolific life, Giambattista Piranesi produced only one design that is called "plan": the *Pianta di ampio magnifico Collegio*. Having been accused by the *Academie de France* of being incapable of producing a proper plan, the Italian responded with the *Collegio* drawing. It looks very much like a plan: lines on paper generated by geometry, *poché* indicating columns and walls, solid and dotted lines indicating stairs, vaults, and beams. It appears to be connected directly to the world of tension and compression, and it is connected—but only insidiously. A close examination reveals that the "building" represented by this single drawing is not an enclosure of stone and wood and plaster but a much more intricate and difficult construction.

It is a plan divorced from gravity, a section through an object constructed with ideas, an *ampio* (both ample and diffuse) *Collegio* (a college, an assembly). It is a translucent slice, a window; also a slicer—Piranesi's critical knife, cutting open, laying bare, revealing. The section, the having-been-cut, is itself an instrument of incision: it is both the plane of inscription and the plane of incision. The section is a connection between worlds. The section delineates "here" and serves as an interface between "theres."

So, what is "here"? In the gravity-world we read (both in the architectural metalanguage of the plan and in Piranesi's inscription) a text composed of bits and pieces of conventional building from the Greco-Roman tradition: a critical text commenting on Baroque architecture. But what is "here" in the grand field? What do we read when the plan becomes only what we really have here: a network of tiny canals of engraver's ink sucked up and frozen on a sheet of paper?

Geometry. A series of concentric rings not quite contained by a square. Some geometric barnacles clinging to the periphery. The rings are sliced into eight equal pieces by a web of eight radial swaths that gesture toward intersection at an unmarked center. We focus on this wheel, this window; the power of the instrument seems to reside here. Circles cut by *V*s. Eight *V*s in a circle.

⟨[T]he strategy of criticism is located in the object of criticism . . . It is not necessary to introduce methods to read this text: the method is in the text. The text is its own criticism, its own explication, its own application. This is not a special case: it is one that is perfectly generalizable. Why should there be dichotomy between texts, between the ones that operate and the ones that are operated upon? There are texts, and that is all.⟩²

⟨Snicker-snack!⟩³ ⟨[T]his 'scission' . . . marks the arbitrary insertion of the letter-opener by which the reading process is opened up indifferently here or there, the cutting edge of writing which begins with the reading of some sequence clipped out from there or here, the chancy but necessary repetition of the already-thereness of some (other) text, the sharp blade of decision.⟩⁴

With two incisions in V-configuration, we can remove a first piece. Call it VARIORUM. With this V-section removed the thing collapses into a tangled mess like the "lace apron" of a cat on the dissection table. But the two incisions yield two ends. Grasp them in two hands and hold the slice up to the light. Seven sections of section—read them left to right or right to left. Call them:

VAGARY INVAGINATION VESSEL VOID VERGE VIOLATION INTERVAL

VARIORUM

⟨[1 variorum of various persons . . . in the phrase *cum notis variorum* with the notes of various persons] 1: an edition of a text esp. of a classical author with notes by different persons; 2: an edition of a publication containing variant readings of the text⟩⁵

Aighuh—and no manes and horses' trot? butt, butt
Of earth, birds spreading harps, two manes a pair
Of birds, each bird a word, a streaming gut
Trot, trot—? No horse is here, no horse is there?
Says you! Then I–fellow me, airs! we'll make
Wood horse, and recognize it with our words–
Not it–nine less two!—as many as take
To make a dead man purple in the face,
Full dress to rise and circle thru a pace
Trained horses–in latticed orchards, (switch!) birds.
—Louis Zukofsky, "*A*"⁶

---

2. Michael Serres, *Hermes: Literature, Science, Philosophy*, ed. Josué V. Harari and David F. Bell (Baltimore: The Johns Hopkins University Press, 1983), 38.
3. Lewis Carroll, "Jabberwocky," *Through the Looking Glass* (New York: New American Library, 1960), 136.
4. Jacques Derrida, *Dissemination*, trans. Barbara Johnson (Chicago: University of Chicago Press, 1981), 300–01.
5. *Webster's Third New International Dictionary of the English Language Unabridged*, 1967.
6. Louis Zukofsky, "*A*" (Berkeley and Los Angeles: Univ. of CA Press, (1978).

VAGARY

⟨1 archaic: journey, excursion, tour; 2 archaic: an aimless digression; 4: a departure from the expected, normal, or logical order or course⟩[7]

⟨The path of the carding wheels is straight and crooked.⟩[8]

⟨On old Olympus' towering top, a Finn and German viewed ...⟩[9]

The tenth, and longest, pair of cranial nerves is called *vagus*—wandering, wandering from the back of the head down into the core of the belly. The word is akin to "prevaricate," to walk knock-kneed, with crooked feet. A person who ambulates with crooked feet leaves tracks of non-convergent Vs. She is like crooked footed Oedipus whose tracks formed a map of his life: two distinct lines, the line of seeking the cause of devastation and the line of being the cause of devastation, heading toward convergence. Oedipus, unwitting prevaricator, walked in V-fashion and lived two lives that met in V-fashion. At the point of convergence—the focal point, the vanishing point—Oedipus jabbed out his eyes. Seeing—constructing relationships among the signs—was for him the interface—a transverse section—between collection and speculation, between in-front-of-the-eyes perception and behind-the-eyes perception.

⟨V at the age of thirty-three ... had found love at last in her peregrinations through (let us be honest) a world if not created then at least described to its fullest by Karl Baedeker of Leipzig. This is a curious country, populated only by a breed called 'tourists.' Its landscape is one of inanimate monuments and buildings ... More than this it is two-dimensional, as is the Street, as are the pages and maps of those little red handbooks.⟩[10]

⟨Follow the tour guide/ accurately./ When you will have reached/ the place where the hotel is located (it is the best/ existing hotel)/ you'll see that you/ have found absolutely/—go on calmly—nothing./ The tour guide does not lie.⟩[11]

⟨lens your dappled yeye here, mine's presbyoperian.⟩[12]

---

7. *Webster's Third New International Dictionary of the English Language Unabridged*, 1967.
8. Heraclitus, Fragment LXXIV, in Charles Kahn, *The Art and Thought of Heraclitus* (Cambridge: Cambridge University Press, 1983), 63.
9. Part of a mnemonic device for listing the cranial nerves in order of their occurrence.
10 Thomas Pynchon, *V*, (New York: Bantam, 1981), 384.
11. Giorgio Caproni, "Sure Direction," trans. Annaliza Sacca, in *The Literary Review* 28, no. 2 (Winter 1985): 221.
12. James Joyce, *Finnegans Wake* (New York: Viking, 1965), 293.32–294.01.

TOWARDS DESIRING ARCHITECTURE

In front of the focal point, what is seen is *poché*, black spots on the eye. Resident *poché* we call floaters: bits of detritus floating passively in the vitreous humor, like plankton (the wandering ones). Alien *pochés*—Piranesi's drawing, a collection of black spots—held in front of the eye describe a screen or window through which to see.

The section is an eye through which the eye sees. The transmission of information begins at the point of a V, or at the intersection of Vs, at the back of the eye. The section, the *poché*, is in front of the eye, in the eye, at the back of the eye. Behind the eye, it can remain intact—an object seen; it can become a center—an object analyzed; or it can become disseminated—an object, a thrown-in-the-way, cut apart into bits that drift and explore—inquire, seek, ramify, connecting to other bits, forming a new text in which shards of the old object are embedded. ⟨It is this way with sewer stories. They just are. Truth or falsity don't apply.⟩[13]

INVAGINATION
⟨The way up and down is one and the same.⟩[14]

⟨In the world of eternal return the weight of unbearable responsibility lies heavy on every move we make. That is why Nietzsche called the idea of eternal return the heaviest of burdens (*das schwerste Gewicht*). If eternal return is the heaviest of burdens, then our lives can stand out against it in all their splendid lightness. But is heaviness truly deplorable and lightness splendid? The heaviest of burdens crushes us, we sink beneath it, it pins us to the ground. But in the love poetry of every age, the woman longs to be weighed down by the man's body.[15] The heaviest of burdens is therefore simultaneously an image of life's most intense fulfillment. The heavier the burden, the closer our lives come to the earth, the more real and truthful they become. Conversely, the absolute absence of a burden causes man to be lighter than air, to soar into the heights, take leave of the earth and his earthly being, and become only half real, his movements as free as they are insignificant. What then shall we choose? Weight or lightness?⟩[16]

We perceive both space and time telescopically, in Vs. At the point of the V, at the vanishing point, is a connection—perhaps theological, perhaps theosophical, perhaps temporal, perhaps spatial. It is a

---

13. Pynchon, *V*, 108.
14. Heraclitus, Fragment CIII, in Kahn, *Art and Thought*, 75.
15. I cannot resist pointing out that there is at play here an unbearable lightness of received truth. I am fascinated by the absence of the obvious, that is, the gender of those who have revealed what women want.
16. Milan Kundera, *The Unbearable Lightness of Being* (London: Faber and Faber, 1984), 5.

connection between worlds: an omphalos, a Brennschluss point, a vertex. The *Collegio* drawing is a section through such a connection. It is a model of an excluded middle. It is the place where concepts we call "opposing" flow into one another, a critical point of ambiguity, the site of "both/and."

⟨I wonder if I shall fall right through the earth! How funny it'll seem to come out among the people that walk with their heads downwards! The antipathies, I think—⟩[17]

If we step back for a moment into the world of the drawing as a representation of building, we can read Piranesi's clue. Enter this building through one of its portals. Proceed down the undulating, notched axis before you. As you approach the terminus of the axis, you find . . . not a great center-marking rotunda, but an enormous tangle of stairs that carry you right-left-up-down and suddenly you find yourself moving down one of the other seven axes, into the labyrinth of the building. Inevitably, your wanderings will bring you to another axis that will again draw you toward that centerless middle that flings you out again. It is an equivocal center that does not perform its traditional duty of stabilizing the structure. It is an eccentric center. The building is like Stepanova's set for *Tarelkin's Death*: the terrible interrogation machine—sucking in, whirling around, expelling—surrounded by a collection of collapsing and self-reassembling chairs and exploding tables.

⟨Let's pretend the glass has got soft like gauze, so that we can get through. Why, it's turning into a sort of mist now, I declare!⟩[18] It is the site of "both/and," the locus of . . . ⟨extravent intervulve coupling⟩,[19] a doubling, ⟨one world burrowing on another.⟩[20]

Worlds within worlds, tubes within tubes. Connected: square and circle, male and female, rational and irrational, implosion and explosion. Sucking in, whirling around, and expelling—digestion, respiration, reproduction, creative thought. It is a section through a body, a universe, a book.

A spherical cell is violated by a line-driven cell. The tail (the line) breaks off. Information flows. The construction begins. The cell-within-a-cell splits and doubles: one into two into four into eight. Now it is a round, bumpy cluster of cells with a void inside. Blastopore! The outer wall collapses inward at a tiny point. Over the

---

17. Lewis Carroll, *Alice in Wonderland* (New York: New American Library, 1960), 19.
18. Carroll, *Through the Looking Glass*, 129.
19. Joyce, *Finnegans Wake*, 314.20.
20. Ibid., 275.05.

lip of this imploding hole slide streaky layers of differentiated cells—endoderm, mesoderm, notochord. The outside becomes the inside. Gastrulation: invagination, involution, epiboly. Implosion. How we achieve our tube-within-a-tubeness.

We are tubes within tubes (continuous outer-inner surfaces) with intricately articulated interstices—ampio. Systems of cells are woven into a dense textile, filling the spaces between inside and outside surface: hierarchies from bone-muscle-nerve-blood vessel to C HOPKINS CaFe, Mighty good, Naturally Clean[21] to quarks and leptons. A section will reveal: the body—the container—is an architecture in the interval.

⟨He indeed was visited by dreams in which he had shrunk to sub-microscopic size and entered a brain, strolling in through some forehead's pore and into the cul-de-sac of a sweat gland. Struggling out of a jungle of capillaries, there he would finally reach bone; down then through the skull, dura mater, arachnoid, pia mater to the fissure floored sea of cerebrospinal fluid. And there he would float before final assault on the gray hemispheres: the soul./ Nodes of Ranvier, sheath of Schwann, vein of Galen; tiny Stencil wandered all night long among the silent immense lightning bursts of nerve-impulses crossing a synapse; the waving dendrites, the nerve autobahns chaining away to God knew where in receding clusters of end-bulbs. A stranger in this landscape, it never occurred to him to ask whose brain he was in. Perhaps his own.⟩[22]

⟨The Lord whose oracle is in Delphi neither declares nor conceals, but gives a sign.⟩[23]

VESSEL

A vessel is both a container and a conduit, the sea and the ship. It is the disseminated and the instrument of dissemination. Vessels are instruments of flux: information, oxygen, food, antibodies, semen. The drawing may be read as a vas deferens, a deferent[24] vessel: a vessel of difference and deference, a *vas différance*. Standing in for an artificial erection (like Isis's artifice—the other of Daedalus's artifice), it marks the point of exchange, the lip, the rim of the flow. The verge, the place where something is about to happen.

21. A mnemonic device for the constituents of protoplasm: Carbobon, Hydrogen, Oxygen, Phosphorus, Potassium (K), Iodine, etc.
22. Pynchon, *V*, 443. Stencil is Herbert Stencil, the protagonist of *V*, whose name translated into French is *Pochoir*.
23. Heraclitus, Fragment XXXIII, in Kahn, *Art and Thought*, 43.
24. From *Webster's Third*: "Deferent *n*. 1: an imaginary circle surrounding the earth in whose periphery, acc. to Ptolemy, either the celestial body or the center of its epicycle is supposed to move *adj*. 2: serving to carry out or down; deferential."

⟨But in the dynamic space of the living Rocket, the double integral has a different meaning. To integrate here is to operate on a rate of exchange so that time falls away: change is stilled ... 'Meters per second' will integrate to 'meters.' The moving vehicle is frozen, in space, to become architecture, and timeless. It was never launched. It will never fall.⟩[25]

The *rocchetto* is a woman's tool—instrument of textile-making. The erection at Cape Canaveral meets Isis's construction, a woman's tool, at the drawing, perhaps not too surprised at the mirror image it encounters.

⟨[C]onstruct ann aquilittoral dryankle Probe loom! With his primal handstoe in his sole salivarium. Concoct an equo-angular trilitter. (As Rhombulus and Rhebus went building rhomes one day.⟩[26]

Here is the fish bladder, *vesica piscis*, vessel of flux, where male and female, space and time, science and magic, meet. It is a section through *Finnegans Wake* and through the cosmos. Follow Joyce's instructions for perceiving it three-dimensionally—extruding Euclid across the border into the non-Euclidean world, cut a transverse section through that, and you will have Piranesi's construction.

⟨Show that the median, hce che ech, intersecting at royde angles the parilegs of a given obtuse one biscuts the arcs that are in curveachord behind. Brickbaths. The family umbroglia.⟩[27] ⟨till its nether nadir is cortically where (allow me aright to two cute winkles) its naval's napex will have to beandbe.⟩[28]

The hen's letter of *Finnegans Wake*, the disseminated, signifying creation—the sex act and the act of city-building, is the *poché* of the vessel. The letter is *thalatta* is the ladder—Jacob's or Wittgenstein's, the sea and the conduit. The letter is *poché*, black spots scattered; also, systems of *T*'s, trabeation, architecture.

⟨The hidden attunement is better than the obvious one.⟩[29]

⟨peep inside the cerebralised saucepan of this eer illwinded goodfornobody you would see in his house of thoughtsam (was you, that is, decontaminated enough to look discarnate) what a jetsam litterage of convolvuli of times lost or strayed, of lands derelict and of tongues laggin too, longa yamsayore, not only that but, search lighting,

25. Thomas Pynchon, *Gravity's Rainbow* (New York: Bantam Books, 1974), 350.
26. Joyce, *Finnegans Wake*, 286.19–22.
27. Ibid., 283.32–284.04.
28. Ibid., 297.12–14.
29. Heraclitus, Fragment LXXX, in Kahn, *Art and Thought*, 65.

beached, bashed and beaushelled *a la Mer* pharahead into faturity, your own convolvulis pickninnig capman would real to jazztfancy the novo takin place of what stale words whilom were woven with the fitted fairly featly for, so; and equally so, the crame of the whole faustian fustian, whether your launer's lightsome or your soulard's schwearmood, it is that, whenas the swiftshut scareyss of your pupil-teachertaut duplex will hark back to lark to you symibellically, that, though a day be as dense as a decade, no mouth has the might to set a mearbound to the march of a landsmaul, in half a sylb, helf a solb, holf a salb onward the beast of boredom, common sense, lurking gyrographically down inside his loose Eating S.S. collar is gogoing of whisth to you sternly how—Plutonic loveliaks twintt Platonic yearlings—you must, how, in undivided reawlity draw the line somewhawre⟩[30]

⟨The sea is the purest and foulest water: for fish drinkable and life-sustaining; for men undrinkable and deadly.⟩[31]

VOID

The *Collegio* is a circle inscribed in a square. The square is only implied by four corners, four broken isosceles right triangles, four wide *V*s. The square, the created figure, is tacked to the circle, the creator figure, through the empty center, the last of the concentric rings. The omphalos supplements the phallus. The parts of Leonardo's cosmos shift and slide, now aligned on a hole, ⟨The no placelike no timelike absolent.⟩[32]

⟨Can proximity cause vertigo?/ It can. When the north pole comes so close as to touch the south pole, the earth disappears and man finds himself in a void that makes his head spin and beckons him to fall.⟩[33]

The *V*s of the drawing point toward convergence, but do not converge. The vanishing point is indicated, but is not 'on the map.' The world of Kasimir Malevich (the four-dimensional world reached by passing through the vanishing point) may be beyond this hole. The void is the passage between worlds of *n* and *n+1* dimensions. The section is a window; the void is a door.

⟨You can just see a little *peep* of the passage in Looking Glass House, if you leave the door of our drawing-room wide open: and it's very like our passage as far as you can see, only you know it may be quite different on beyond.⟩[34]

30. Joyce, *Finnegans Wake*, 292.13-32.
31. Heraclitus, Fragment LXX, in Kahn, *Art and Thought*, 61.
32. Joyce, *Finnegans Wake*, 609.02.
33. Kundera, *The Unbearable Lightness of Being*, 224.
34. Carroll, *Through the Looking Glass*, 129.

The (strangely) looping stairs define the empty center. It is not hard to see a connection between this drawing and the centerless infinite looping of some of Piranesi's *Carceri*. ⟨Behind these halls with their barred bull's-eyes, we suspect there are other halls just like them, deduced or deducible in every direction. The frail catwalks, the drawbridges in mid-air which almost everywhere double the galleries and the stone staircases, seem to correspond to the same desire to hurl into space all possible curves and parallels. This world closed over itself is mathematically infinite.⟩[35]

The endless repetitive climbing required in *Collegio* center-approaching resembles the Castle-approaching of Kafka's land surveyor; which, as Borges has pointed out, is like the Tortoise-approaching of Achilles; which, as Douglas Hofstadter has pointed out, is like the activity of those who populate the drawings of M. C. Escher; which is something like the stair-climbing of Kerensky in Eisenstein's *October*, a montage sequence inspired by the *Carceri*.

⟨Flop! Your rere gait's creakorheuman bitts your butts disagrees.⟩[36]

⟨Holy-Center-Approaching [, a] ⟨pastime [with] about the same vulnerability to record-breakers as baseball, a sport also well-spidered with white suggestions of the sinister[,]⟩ is soon to be the number one Zonal pastime.⟩[37]

To score, to reach the center, is to make the leap, to traverse the passage between worlds, to fall down the hole, to climb Jacob's ladder—to come to an end that is a beginning. The most powerful, sublime passages are those the other side of which are unknown or unspeakable, in which the void is the middle between known and unknown or speakable and unspeakable. Wittgenstein's *Tractatus*-closing aphorism ("What we cannot speak about we must pass over in silence") is a section—a middle—delineating the border between the unspeakable and language. It is that which language cannot describe described with language. It points out the difficulty of middles—the place where emptiness and intricacy are the same, the place of perplexing (thoroughly woven) emptiness. (The void where the family secrets are encrypted—the "family umbroglio.")

The (void) center does not hold, but the word is used to describe the condition. So the center both holds and does not hold. It is in a holding pattern.

---

35. Marguerite Yourcenar, *The Dark Brain of Piranesi*, trans. Richard Howard (New York: Farrar, Straus and Giroux, 1984), 114.
36. Joyce, *Finnegans Wake*, 214.21–22.
37. Pynchon, *Gravity's Rainbow*, 592 and 593.

⟨In the beginning is the woid, in the muddle is the soundance and thereinofter you're in the unbewised again, vund vulsyvolsy.⟩[38]

⟨It is here you must look, at the center of our galaxy, where all calculations and instruments point to the presence of an enormous bodily mass which however cannot be seen. Spider webs of radiation and gas, perhaps left entangled at the time of the last explosions, prove that in their midst lies one of these so-called holes, now spent like an old crater. All that surrounds us, the wheel of planetary systems and constellations and branches of the milky way, every single thing in our galaxy is pivoted on this implosion plunged inside itself. That is my pole, my mirror, my secret homeland.⟩[39]

VERGE

⟨[me, fr. L. *Virga* twig, rod, streak, stripe—more at whisk] 1a (1): a rod or staff carried as an emblem of authority or as a symbol of office . . . ;b (1): the spindle of a watch balance; esp: a spindle with pallets in an old vertical escapement c: the male intromittent organ of any of various invertebrates . . . ;d (2): a bobbin guide on a lace machine; 2a: something that borders, limits, or bounds . . . ;(2) obs: an enclosing band: *circlet, ring* . . . also: rim, brim . . . ;(7) *horizon* . . . ;(8): the edge of the tiling projecting over the gable of a roof . . . ;b: the point marking the beginning—of a new or different state, condition, or action: brink, *threshold*.⟩[40]

⟨Immortals are mortal, mortals immortal, living the others' death, dead the others' life.⟩[41]

⟨[The equations predicting black holes] have not one but two solutions. In the second solution, the equations yield a "white hole," a center from which energy and matter radiate outward rather than being sucked in as they are in a black hole . . . [A] black hole can be transformed into a white hole by reversing the value of time in the equations . . . If the substance of the universe is being sucked into black holes, it is being spewed out again from white holes in a circular dialectic in which annihilation and rebirth are simply two sides of the same coin.⟩[42]

---

38. Joyce, *Finnegans Wake*, 378.29-31.
39. Italo Calvino, "The Implosion," trans. S. Eugene Scalia, in *The Literary Review* (Winter 1985): 221.
40. *Webster's Third*.
41. Heraclitus, Fragment XCII, in Kahn, *Art and Thought*, 71.
42. N. Katherine Hayles, *The Cosmic Web: Scientific Field Models and Literary Strategies in the Twentieth Century* (Ithaca: Cornell University Press, 1984), 195-196.

⟨Rachel was looking into the mirror at an angle of 45°, and so had a view of the face [of a clock] turned toward the room and the face on the other side, reflected in the mirror; here were time and reverse-time, co-existing, canceling one another exactly out.⟩[43] ⟨Skeletons, carapaces, no matter: her inside too was her outside.⟩[44]

⟨Consider coal and steel. There is a place where they meet. the interface between coal and steel is coal tar. Imagine coal, down in the earth, dead black, no light, the very substance of death. Death ancient, prehistoric, species *we will never see again*. Growing older, blacker, deeper, in layers of perpetual night. Above ground, the steel rolls out fiery, bright. But to make steel the coal tars, darker and heavier, must be taken from the original coal. Earth's excrement, purged out for the ennoblement of shining steel.⟩[45]

VIOLATION

⟨Behind all European faiths, religious and political, we find the first chapter of Genesis, which tells us that the world was created properly, that human existence is good, and that we are therefore entitled to multiply. Let us call this basic faith a *categorical agreement with being* ... [T]he aesthetic ideal of the categorical agreement with being is a world in which shit is denied and everyone acts as though it did not exist. This aesthetic ideal is called *kitsch*.⟩[46]

Piranesi's architecture is contaminated. It is *kitsch* (if one will allow the anachronism) violated by bits of detritus, bits of digested material. It is a metacommentary on the paradox of kitsch: Kitsch is centered around an absence. This center is unspeakable and unapproachable because it (the tube within a tube) is a vessel of—what else?—excrement, violation of the ideal. In persistent avoidance (a-voidance) of shit, shit becomes the focus, the center. Rupture—void—the center and it "hits the fan," is disseminated, making a dappled thing: mottled, motley, dark-spotted, *ampio*. A rocket is propelled this way, by the expulsion of its own waste.

⟨Imagine that you have swallowed a cylindrical mirror. Upright, bigger than you are ... This glass column traverses, dominates, regulates, and reflects, in its numerous polysemy, the entire set of squares. / It is a Tower of Babel in which multiple languages and forms of writing bump into each other or mingle with each other, constantly being transformed and engendered through their most

---

43. Pynchon, *V*, 36.
44. Ibid., 426.
45. Pynchon, *Gravity's Rainbow*, 194.
46. Kundera, *The Unbearable Lightness of Being*, 248.

unreconcilable otherness to each other, an otherness which is strongly affirmed, too, for plurality here is bottomless and is not lived as negativity, with any nostalgia for lost unity.⟩[47]

In a film originally and significantly called *Edge City* (re-released as *Repo Man*), there is a character called Miller—repo-lot watchdog, man of garbage—who rides buses over rhizomatous pathways. Miller is an advocate of Dioretix, a mind-over-matter pop movement that, like its homophonic counterpart, voids weight, producing lightness. The hot car, in Miller's hands, becomes a virtual rocket.

⟨The question: to explode or to implode, would it again come up? Absorbed by the vortex of this galaxy, would one reappear in other times and other skies? To sink here into profound silence, to express oneself there in flaming shrieks of another language? To absorb here evil and good like a sponge in the shade, to gush out there like a dazzling jet, to spread, expend, lose oneself?⟩[48]

⟨Even in Florence . . . he had noted an obsession with bodily incorporating little bits of inert matter.⟩[49] ⟨Flip!⟩[50]

We can't see V-particles, but we know they've been there, tiny collision bits leaving little V-shaped tracks. The angles of history.

⟨The fairest order in the world is a heap of random sweepings.⟩[51]

INTERVAL

⟨Flep!⟩[52]

The word results from the coupling of *inter* (between, among) and *vallum* (palisade or wall, from *vallus*, post or stake). (This suggests that an architecture of the interval is both among the walls and among—in the interstices between—the posts, or poles, totem or otherwise.) "Interval" literally means "between the walls." It suggests a place that might be occupied, a space. It elicits a number of images. One is the place between or among the walls of a labyrinth—the place of wandering, of seeking, of exploratory movement that might be mapped.

Maps themselves exist in intervals. Maps are not what they purport to be. They have something to do with representing places—geography; but they are as importantly about time—chronology,

---

47. Derrida, *Dissemination*, 341.
48. Calvino, "The Implosion," 215.
49. Pynchon, *V*, 459.
50. Joyce, *Finnegans Wake*, 213.22.
51. Heraclitus, Fragment CXXV, in Kahn *Art and Thought*, 85.
52. Joyce, *Finnegans Wake*, 213.23.

what we do, how we move through. Maps, then, exist in the interval between the walls of geography and chronology. They exist in the interval between reality and those who order the experience of it.

The schema of a map's generation—that experience of reality—is embedded in the map itself. This suggests a second image of interval: the place within the walls of an object in which lie the tools of that object's generation. This kind of object, then, contains the schema, or tools, with which it was made. It is like the Ideal Palace of Cheval or Carlo Scarpa's Abatellis Palace in Palermo, for which working drawings were made on the walls themselves, then covered over with plaster.[53]

A third image is the gap between boundaries, the place where the edges of things come close to touching. The place of architecture seems to be here in these places (as well as in its conventional disciplinary capsule, which rather sheepishly embeds itself in an imagined wall between art and science). This architecture is not disciplinary, but interdisciplinary. It seeps out of its capsule and bleeds into the interstices, the intervals among the dissolving walls of other capsules: philosophy, science, literature. Architecture not in a capsule, but in a soup.[54]

⟨Stencil sketched the entire history of V. that night and strengthened a long suspicion. That it did add up only to the recurrence of an initial and a few dead objects.⟩[55]

⟨Graspings: wholes and not wholes, convergent and divergent, consonant dissonant, from all things one and from one thing all.⟩[56]

> Light wave and quantum, we have good proof both exist:
> Our present effort is to see how this is: to
> Perfect the composition of a two-point view
> ...
> Build it.
>
> —Louis Zukofsky, "*A*"

---

53. From Marco Frascari, "Carlo Scarpa in Magna Graecia: The Abatellis Palace in Palermo," *AA Files*, no. 9 (Summer 1985): 9.
54. The preceding paragraphs are taken from "Interval," the text of a talk I gave at Yale, published in *Art Papers* (July/August, 1985).
55. Pynchon, *V*, 419.
56. Heraclitus, Fragment CXXIV, in Kahn, *Art and Thought, 85. Kahn* points out that the initial word *[syllapsies]* has by others been translated "connections" and "assemblages," and that for Aristotle the word could have meant "conception" or "pregnancy."

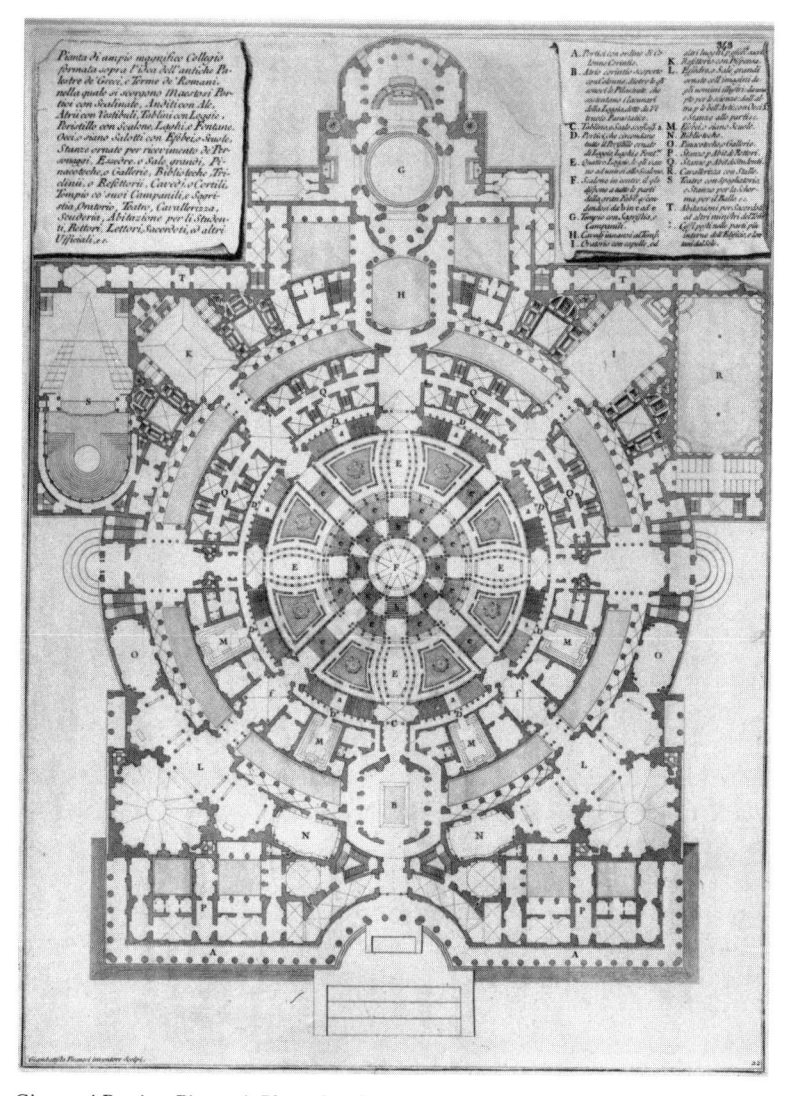

Giovanni Battista Piranesi, Plan of an Imaginary Seat of Learning, 1750. Etching

POSTSCRIPT: TAUPOLOGIE OF THE *COLLEGIO*

The ghosts of many fathers will be conjured with the caveat that this postscript demands an awareness of an interweaving of speech and writing, a muddying of the distinction between the visual and the verbal. They will not be named—yet.

A BEGINNING

Taupologie is homophonic with and similar to, yet different from, topology. *Taupologie* is the name of the activity of *la taupe*[57]— the mole—a small, soft creature with hidden ears who doesn't see very well and who tunnels about in the dark. Webster gives us other definitions of mole: a congenital [marking a beginning] dark spot on a surface; one who works in the dark; a massive work formed of masonry and large stones or earth laid in the sea [*la mer(e)*] as a pier or breakwater; an abnormal mass in the uterus, especially when containing fetal tissues [marking a beginning]; a gram molecule [a little bit of something]. This constellation of structures about a four-letter word is typical of the activity of the webster, who is concerned with the activity of web-making. The one who is concerned with the activity of the mole, the one who operates in dark soil, will be called a mole-ster. The activity of the mole-ster is connected to topology, which has to do with holes and ruptures in things.

ANOTHER BEGINNING

The formidable ghost of Walter Benjamin, with his text on *Ursprung* (origin) in hand, has already been conjured. In his "children's nursery"[58] (that messy cacophonous place), one might hear a nursery rhyme:

Here's the tale of Michael Finnegan.
He grew whiskers on his chinnegan.
He grew fat and then grew thin again.
Poor old Michael Finnegan. Begin again.
(And so on . . .)

Michael Finnegan is like the bearded father in an illustration from the *Chymica Vannus dell'Alchimia o la scienza sognata*. In the picture, a father/king is on the verge of devouring his son—a representation of primary material devouring and spewing itself back out, growing fat and thin again in a never-ending cycle. This calls to mind another Finnegan, and a whole slew of fathers, the giant a-gents of history, dying and waking, rising and falling, growing fat and thin, all asking the question, "Which came first, the chicken or the egg?" James Joyce's text bears the influence of the strong poetic wisdom of a father of both Joyce and Piranesi, Giambattista Vico.

Edward Said (in *Beginnings: Intention and Method*) wrote: "[Vico] is the first philosopher of beginnings, not because he was the first in time to think as he did . . . but because for him a beginning is at once never given and always indefinite or divined and yet always

---

57. An underminer introduced by Hélène Cixous and Catherine Clément in *The Newly Born Woman* (*La jeune née*), trans. Betsy Wing (Manchester: Manchester University Press, 1986), 65.
58. Walter Benjamin, *The Origin of German Tragic Drama* (1928), trans. John Osborne (London: New Left Books, 1985), 188.

asserted at considerable expense."[59] Vico's beginning is a Joycean "begidding"—a begetting of giddy beginnings—a biting of the apple. Vico's world "begins among stones, rocks, frogs, and cicadas, rather like Yeats' 'foul rag-and-bone shop of the heart'. This is quite another world from Plato's realm of forms or from Descartes' clear and distinct ideas."[60] It is like the "children's nursery" or Joyce's House O'Shea or O'Shame, with its[61]

> warped flooring ... persianly literatured with burst loveletters, telltale stories, stickyback snaps, doubtful eggshells, bouchers, flints, borers, puffers, amygdaloid almonds, rindless raisins, alphybettyformed verbage, vivlical viasses, ompiter dictas, visus umbique, ahems and ahahs, imeffible tries at speech unasyllabled, you owe mes, eyoldhums, fluefoul smut, fallen lucifers, vertas which had served, showered ornaments, borrowed brogues, reversibles jackets, black-eye lenses, family jars, falsehair shirts, Godforsaken scapulars, never-worn breeches, cutthroat ties, counterfeit franks, best intentions, curried notes, upset latten tintacks, unused mill and stumpling stones, twisted quills, painful digests, magnifying wineglasses, solid objects cast at goblins, once current puns, quashed quotatoes, messes of mottage, unquestionable issue papers, seedy ejaculations,

and no doubt the gargantuan ghost of Rabelais dancing diabolically in the rubble.

Vico recognized no distinction between theory and practice. In his text are braided together speculations on the cycles of history and descriptions of (to paraphrase and parody Said) the primitive mothers copulating with their men in caves. (Please note, copulating—like moles—in caves, not in primitive huts, which effectively killed this activity.)

The primitive hut is the house of my fathers. But there is, here, the beginning of an intrusive presence in this house:[62]

> She transforms, she acts: the old culture will soon be the new. She is mixed up in dirty things; she has no cleanliness phobia—the proper housecleaning attacks that hysterics sometimes suffer. She handles filth, manipulates wastes, buries placentas, and burns the cauls of newborn babies for luck. She makes

---

59. Edward Said, *Beginnings: Intention and Method* (New York: Columbia University Press, 1985), 350.
60. Ibid., 348.
61. Joyce, *Finnegans Wake*, 183.08—23.
62. Cixous and Clément, *The Newly Born Woman*, 36.

partial objects useful, puts them back in circulation properly. What a fine mess![63]
To make partial objects circulate . . . At about the same time that the Abbaye (the Father) Laugier is drawing the line of rationality between the primitive hut and the immutable laws of architecture, a literally phallic architecture, there is, just to the south and east, a delirious operative at work, scratching dark spots on a surface, making a massive work of masonry and large stones, like a Cyclops (who doesn't see very well) making an abnormal mass. A "darkbrained"[64] individual incises the canals of an eight-legged critter, an ample, diffuse, and magnificent assemblage, the work of a mole-ster.

It is Piranesi's *Pianta di ampio magnifico Collegio*, an image of what might be were a slice taken through a nonexistent, non-synthesized building. It is an "organism that *pretend[s]* to have a centrality but that never achieve[s] one."[65] It is the center, where we expect a great signifying void—the logic of the rotunda—that throws us. (It throws us quite literally—shuttling us—back out into the periphery of the building—via a subversive apparatus of stairs which push at the limits of building sense and throw the logic of the rest into question and into motion.) The *Collegio* is an assemblage of crypts, glands, follicles, vessels, and valves accommodating, checking, and diverting endless flow; a generative section that will not be extruded, will not obey the tyranny of linear time; mole-work bearing the trace of the tarantella, the activity of hysterics at the mercy of their motile voids. A mercurial vessel. A *taupologie* machine: a "wholemole millwheeling vicociclometer"[66] that "secretly undermines the laws to which it pretends to subject itself."[67] An hysterical document, it is a representation of the "psychical house"[68] that Freud built—a house with a strange apparatus in the middle: an intricate void, where the (family) history is encrypted (inscribed and secreted). "A cataleptic mithyphallic! was this *Totem Fulcrum Est* Ancestor yu hald in Dies Eirae where no spider webbeth . . . ?"[69] Held-In Desire, Halled-In

---

63. Betsy Wing, the translator of *La jeune née*, points out that the phrase "*En voila du propre!*" (In English, "What a fine mess!") is used in the text in places where that which is "appropriate" is called into question. Ibid., 167.
64. A reference to the title of Marguerite Yourcenar's essay, "The Dark Brain of Piranesi."
65. Manfredo Tafuri, *The Sphere and the Labyrinth: Avant-Gardes and Architecture from Piranesi to the 1970s*, trans. Pellegrino d'Acierno and Robert Connolly (Cambridge: MIT Press, 1987), 27.
66. Joyce, *Finnegans Wake*, 614.27.
67. Tafuri, *The Sphere and the Labyrinth*, 31.
68. Cixous and Clément, *The Newly Born Woman*, 56.
69. Joyce, *Finnegans Wake*, 481.04–05. A decoding of this passage is appropriate here. A cataleptic (a state of paralysis in which body parts remain wherever they are placed)

Desire. The *Collegio* is a paradox: a vital vivisection of a vessel of the patriarchal symbolic order dancing off the poisons of that order that circulate through its body, it is a momentary catalepsy of an architecture of desire.

At this point, the signifier "mole-ster" secretly appropriates (secretes) a third syllable, invades the void. The daughter, who is excluded from the house of "history, locked up tight between father and son,"[70] "annoys," "disturbs," and "makes indecent advances."[71] The mole-ster tunnels back around in a topological move, like a Klein worm, and becomes the Molester. She is wicked: "morally bad," "vicious," "disgustingly unpleasant."[72]

The "Wicked Architect"[73] attempts "to close the distance between the written act and the committed act,"[74] to occupy the "void which cannot be represented," the place where "the drawing always stops,"[75] the space between the drawing and the construction—the house—with intricate, intersecting interstices. It is a network of genealogical lines. "History as a 'project of crisis', then."[76] "[Hystery] is not that which cloaks itself in indisputable 'philological proofs', but that which recognizes itself as an 'unsafe building'."[77]

Mano Freddo Taffiare, you guzzling geezer with frigid hand, writing "delirious constructions" yourself, can I bite you *senza fare il passo piu lungo della gamba*—without making a step longer than my leg, falling into the void? *La tarantola* is restless.[78]

---

or catalytic (describing material used in a chemical reaction to increase its rate, the material itself remaining unchanged by the reaction) misce-phallic/mis-cephalic/myth of phallic (plus Mithraic—ancient male mystery cult—and Mithridates—king of ancient times who regularly ingested small quantities of poison, thereby gaining immunity to it—a *Pharmakon*). Was this *Totem Fulcrum Est* (the family emblem is the bed/post/phallus, the totem is—after all—a pole) Ancestor yu hald in *Dies Eirae* (you halled/hailed/held in this area/day or ire/day of Ireland/desire) where no spider webbeth (a proper, clean—*propre*—place).

70. Cixous and Clément, *The Newly Born Woman*, 56.
71. *Webster's Third*, 545.
72. Ibid., 1020.
73. A reference to Tafuri's essay on Piranesi in *The Sphere and the Labyrinth*.
74. Ibid., 17.
75. Aldo Rossi, *A Scientific Autobiography*, trans. Lawrence Venuti (Cambridge: MIT Press, 1981), 24.
76. Tafuri, "The Historical Project," in *The Sphere and the Labyrinth*, 13.
77. Ibid., 12.
78. It is perhaps abundantly apparent that the primary father in question here is Manfredo Tafuri, the coiner of the phrase, "delirious constructions" (Tafuri, op. cit., 11). *Mano* (hand), *freddo* (cold), *taffiare* (to guzzle). The English equivalent of *fare il passo piu longa della gamba* (to take a step longer than the leg) is "to bite off more than one can chew." *Avere la tarantola* (to have the tarantula) is the same as "having ants in one's pants."

Mes pères, je vous lis difficilement. (Je vous lit difficilement.) I misread you. I miswrite you. I molest you.

ANOTHER BEGINNING

Julia Kristeva has written: "As capitalist society is being economically and politically choked to death, discourse is wearing thin and heading for collapse at a more rapid rate than ever before . . . Only one language grows more and more contemporary: the equivalent . . . of the language of *Finnegans Wake*."[79] *Finnegans Wake* is a map for an architecture of desire, in which "desire causes the signifier to appear as heterogeneous and, inversely, indicates heterogeneity through and across the signifier."[80] The *Collegio* is a mark of an architecture of floating signifiers, an architecture that "sanction[s] the definitive divorce of architectural *signs* from their signifieds."[81]

If one makes a reentry into the *Collegio* through one of its grand portals, clearly inscribed in accordance with the immutable symbolic order of architectural drawings, one will get the picture, the image, but the apparatus will elude. It is far more "joyceful" to enter this text by sliding in along the path of the inscribing or incising tool, sliding through a tear in the old curtains in the back of the theater (be it the magic theater or the operating theater, the domain of the magician or the surgeon), then to circulate, molelike, within the dark areas.

---

79. Julia Kristeva, *Desire in Language: A Semiotic Approach to Literature and Art*, trans. Alice Jardine, Thomas Gora, and Leon Roudiez, ed. Leon Roudiez (Oxford: Blackwell, 1980), 92.
80. Ibid., 116.
81. Tafuri, *The Sphere and the Labyrinth*, 40.

CATHERINE INGRAHAM

LINES AND LINEARITY:
PROBLEMS IN ARCHITECTURAL THEORY

We assume we now live relatively effortlessly on earth, an assumption that depends on our ability to pass through the "membrane of human artifice"[1] we see as an inconsequential separation of human beings from other species (from the life of the planet). I want to suggest, conversely, that human beings exist always effort*fully* through these artifices—through architecture in the broadest sense. The humanist mode of inquiry that led us to the idea of effortless inhabitation believed in our inability to speak of something called the "human condition." Hannah Arendt, among others, situates this condition both historically and philosophically. Humanism granted an idealized autonomy to the human subject—an autonomy that depends on what Jacques Lacan calls the "consciousness-perception system" and the "reality principle." According to Lacan, this prin-

---

1. These words belong to Hannah Arendt who begins *The Human Condition* with remarks on the first space flight: "This event, second to no other . . . would have been greeted with unmitigated joy if it had not been for the uncomfortable military and political circumstances attached to it . . . The immediate reaction, expressed on the spur of the moment, was relief about the first 'step toward escape from man's imprisonment to the earth.'" For Arendt, the "modern age" is signaled by mankind's wish to exchange the conditions of life on earth "where humans can breathe without effort and artifice" for "something he has made himself." See: Hannah Arendt, *The Human Condition* (Chicago: The University of Chicago Press, 1958), 1-5. If, as I suggest, there is no such thing as "effortless inhabitation," then space flight, with its artificial life support systems, is a structural extension, rather than a rupture, of our artificed status on earth. One might say that human beings already live within a world they have "made themselves."

ciple "is the expression of a scientific prejudice most hostile to the dialectic of knowledge."[2] This "reality principle" relies, at least in part, on a linear—that is, a direct and unmediated—relationship between the human self and the world landscape within which this self operates. This relationship is fixed as primordially human and includes the possibility of a will acting meaningfully on the world. Under humanist principles, the world is a landscape separate from human beings but available to them through linear means of representation.[3] Representative systems are dependent on principles of connection and adequation that assume the world can be translated, word for word, form for form, into a representation. The trope of translation, traditionally, is the map. The humanist world is mapped rather than constructed.[4]

But there are, of course, many problems here. Recent theoretical developments have made it difficult to regard the complex sedimentation of culture as a resolved condition. Further, no sooner does a landscape present itself to us (an aerial photograph of Amazonian rain forests; Le Corbusier's diagrams of the *Ville Radieuse*; a city, garden, or vista) than we become aware—under the influence, to be sure, of what we now know as the critique of representation—of the apparatus that supports and makes possible that landscape. To quickly summarize a complex and far from homogenous body of

2. See: Jacques Lacan, "The mirror stage as formative of the function of the I as revealed in psychoanalytic experience," *Ecrits* (New York: Norton Publishing Company, 1977), 1–7.
3. Methods of translation from the world "as it is" to the world represented in art or science depend not only on the drawing of lines, but also on linear thinking, which Derrida would oppose to the "pluri-dimensional symbolic thought" argued for by poststructural philosophy. See Jacques Derrida, *Of Grammatology*, trans. Gayatri Spivak (Baltimore: Johns Hopkins University Press, 1976), 86. Perspective, for example, has been seen for centuries as an appropriate model for optically representing the way we see; triangulation as an appropriate mode of measuring the irregular landscape; intention as an appropriate description of how our will intersects with the world. All of these are linear modes of translation. For further discussion of (the lines of) optics and visuality in architecture see John Whiteman's unpublished paper "Visual Resistance" (Chicago: Chicago Institute for Architecture and Urbanism, 1990).
4. As is evident, I am using the word "construction" in opposition to the word "map." This relies on the canonical opposition between something created and something discovered, something built or something found. In fact, if we look very closely at cartography on the one hand, and, say, the architectural plan on the other, it is clear that map-making is as much a constructed, indeed designed, "plan" as an architectural plan is a type of map. For the constructions of cartography see J.B. Harley, "Maps, Knowledge and Power," *The Iconography of Landscape: Essays on the symbolic representation, design and use of past environments* (Cambridge: Cambridge University Press, 1985), 277–312. In a different vein, see Svetlana Alpers, *The Art of Describing: Dutch Art in the Seventeenth Century* (Chicago: University of Chicago Press, 1984), especially ch. 4–5.

Carlo Scarpa: Facade of the Banca Populare di Verona. The grille, interior

critical work, critiques of representation focus on fundamental assumptions about the act of representation, in particular the assumption that mimesis (imitation of the world) is possible. By pointing to the ever-present structure of the frame, the lens, the word, the apparatuses of representation, this critique suggests that the "world represented" is the *only* world, since it is impossible to know the world outside of its representations. On the one hand, we would not have the category of "landscape" were it not for its representation in photography, writing, drawing, planning, gardening, painting, mapping, and architecture, and this representation is never free of ideological or mechanical equipment. On the other hand, we would not have the category of "real world" were it not for its contrapuntal relation to representation. The oppositions traditionally governing the relationship between ourselves and the very idea of the world such as conceptual/material, intelligible/sensible are not dissolved under this critique. One might say, rather, that the space of division between these opposition is enlarged in order to be scrutinized more closely.[5]

In effect, we cannot coherently imagine a landscape free from the constraints of a frame.[6] The frame of a painting, airplane window, camera lens, printed margin, and also the frames of political and

---

5. For an important discussion of the "space of division," see Jeffrey Kipnis, "Twisting the Separatrix," *AAFiles*, (London), in press.
6. It will bear remembering that landscaping is a word that carries within itself an improper and architectural (as well as a proper and nautical) etymology of the noun "scape," a "stem bearing fructification and no leaves," or, in a more active sense, the

cultural forces, are all equally governing. Even when flying machines or measuring machines (i.e., for surveying) were in a primitive state or absent altogether, the act of seeing a landscape was no less determined by its frame. The view of the measurer, geometer, urban planner, architect, explorer, traveler, writer, or map-maker is an artificial attention in motion and always machined.[7] Once we become aware of the frame, which I am using here to cover a wide range of both ideological and mechanical governances, our assumptions about a linear translation between the so-called "world itself" and its representation become problematic. In fact, one might even say our assumption about the idea of translation itself is dedicated to keeping inviolate the function of the "linearity" on which it depends.[8] Although we constantly invoke this linearity—often as the "line" of passage and division, the "threshold" or boundary condition—we generally cross over, rather than into, the line itself.

In architecture—and it is architecture that ultimately interests me here—one might suspect that the condition of linearity has a special, perhaps more revealed, position since architecture initially presents itself through the economy and apparatus of the line and an ideal linearity. That the discipline of architecture defines its boundaries and design capacities according to the workings of orthogonality— strictly defined, the "right-angledness" of the line—seems indisputable. Modes of representation in architecture, drawing and model-building for example, are the literal examples of this dedication to orthogonality, but even in epistemological accounts of its own artistic practice, architecture depends on the orthogonalities of

escape of a radical stem from its base, like the shaft of a feather or the springing curve of a column from a base. See *The Concise Oxford Dictionary* (Oxford: Oxford University Press, 1972). The "(e)scape" of the land into a "landscape" suggests what one might call a "radical stem of composition." This stem is traditionally the "straight" one of mimesis. But as I suggest eventually, vis-à-vis the line, this stem is actually the radical root that in Derridean terms has always already divided and spread beyond the reach of mimesis.

7. I want to invoke, for their bluntness as much as their content, Derrida's words about perception: "As to perception, I should say that once I recognized it as a necessary conservation. I was extremely conservative. Now I don't know what perception is and I don't believe anything like perception exists. Perception is precisely a concept, a concept of an intuition or of a given originating from the thing itself, present itself in its meaning, independently from language, from the system of reference. And I believe that perception is interdependent with the concept of origin and of center and consequently whatever strikes at the metaphysics of which I have spoken strikes also at the very concept of perception. I don't believe that there is any perception." See Jacques Derrida, "Structure, Sign and Play," *The Structuralist Controversy* (Baltimore: Johns Hopkins University Press, 1975), 247–272.

8. For an excellent discussion of the issue of "translation" in architecture see Mark Wigley, "The Production of Babel, the Translation of Architecture," in *Assemblage* 8, (Cambridge: MIT Press, 1989).

intention, creativity, and intuition. However, in spite of, or perhaps because of, the power of orthogonality in architecture, the subject of "linearity"—the system enabled by the line that underlies representation—does not make itself known easily. Indeed, it would have been naive to have imagined that it would, since the very self-evidence of the line in architecture guarantees its complexity.

There is, at the very least, a problem in speaking meaningfully of the architectural "line" as if it were a conceptual possibility—an entity available to the act of conception. The line seems more an apparatus than a concept, since its tacit role is to enable other conceptual functions.[9] To give a precise conceptual direction to a discussion of the line is, paradoxically, to be implicated in linear strategies that keep the line itself invisible. As a subject, the line must be outlined—given a shape or character—and it is precisely at the moment when the line takes a shape that it eludes our grasp. Unlike Platonic solids that underlie an idealized geometry, the line is neither ideal nor solid except as it serves other ideal and solid figures. In architecture, it is the grounding of geometries and conceptual material and, simultaneously, without any geometric or conceptual character itself. The line is the means by which architecture displays its conceptual accretions and is therefore at the end of the act of design. And yet it is impossible to design anything without thinking the line itself first. So the line is also a kind of originary marking apparatus whose genealogy is written into the history of geometry, a geometry itself constructed inside a "geometrico-mathematical horizon"[10] that defines the line as pure extension without breadth or depth, without dimension.

---

9. Aldo Rossi remarks on how the word "apparatus" in quotidian Italian phrases such as *apparecchiare la tavola* (to set the table, arrange it, prepare it) and *apparecchio alla morte* (the preparation for death) suggests a table of operation or theater or space of preparation. See Aldo Rossi, *A Scientific Autobiography* (Cambridge: MIT Press, 1985), 4–6. Rossi wants to claim the power of this space of preparation for architecture. The apparatus of architecture, for Rossi, stands for an entire economy of presentation. I want to retain some of the force of this idea while suggesting that the traditional concepts of apparatus and landscape are complicitous in keeping architecture "before the fact" of the linearity it employs to prepare the ground for its own performances.
10. The words "geometrico-mathematical horizon" are from Derrida's introduction to Husserl's *Origin of Geometry*. (See the following section of my essay.) In this work Derrida first marks out many of the strategies he will subsequently use in his deconstruction of western metaphysics. The most recognizable is the critique of the concept of "origin." Derrida points out that the distinctions Husserl depends on for separating geometry from earlier mathematical practices—that is, for giving it an *origin*—are already at work in those earlier practices. The "always already" structure informing Derrida's discussion of Husserl appears later in his critique of writing, particularly in *Of Grammatology*. See: Jacques Derrida, intro. to Edmund Husserl, *Origin of Geometry* (Lincoln: University of Nebraska Press, 1989).

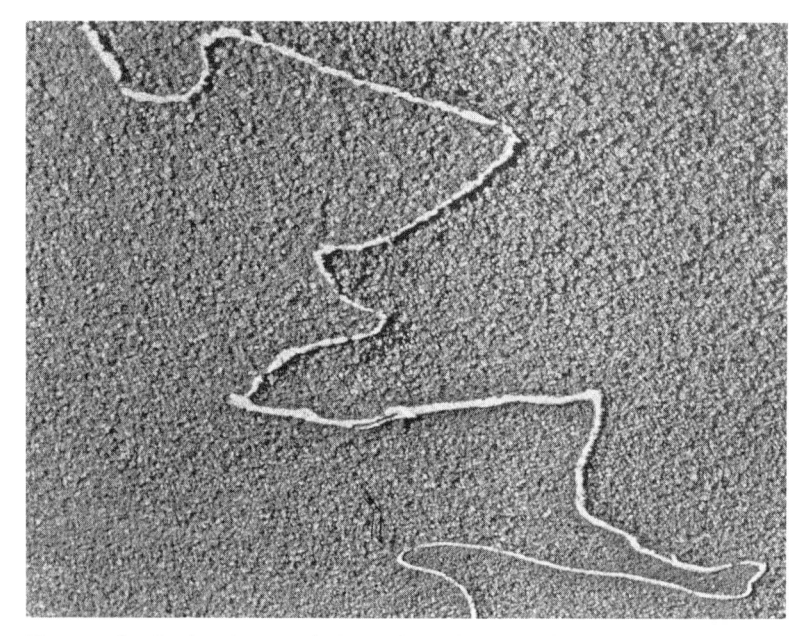

Photograph of a river in a tropical rain forest from an advertisement for the 1990 *Alexander World Atlas*. This new cartography series claims to "show the world as it is."

As Jacques Derrida begins to show in his critique of Edmund Husserl's *Origin of Geometry*, the ideality of geometry—and with it, the ideality of the line—is not a "quantum leap" in the history of understanding. For Husserl the question of the ideal object—geometry—concerns the history of the multiple variations of geometric forms in mathematics. Husserl argues that before the exactitude of forms appeared (that is, before the origin of geometry) "an essential form becomes recognizable through a method of variation." As Derrida summarizes this remark:

> By imaginary variation we can obtain inexact but pure morphological types: 'roundness,' for example, *under* which is *constructed* the geometrical ideality of the 'circle.' In a pregeometrical world, the ideal shapes we attain are not the geometrically 'pure' shapes which can be inscribed in ideal space—'pure' bodies, 'pure' straight lines, 'pure' planes, other 'pure' figures, and the movements and deformations which occur in 'pure' figures.[11]

---

11. Husserl, *Origin of Geometry*, 123-24 (Derrida's italics). It is important to remember that Derrida is investigating the "pregeometrical" account of ideal forms in Husserl. This "pure ideality" is of a sensible order, he remarks, and must be distinguished from the "pure geometrical ideality, which in itself is released from all sensible or imaginative intuitiveness."

LINES AND LINEARITY

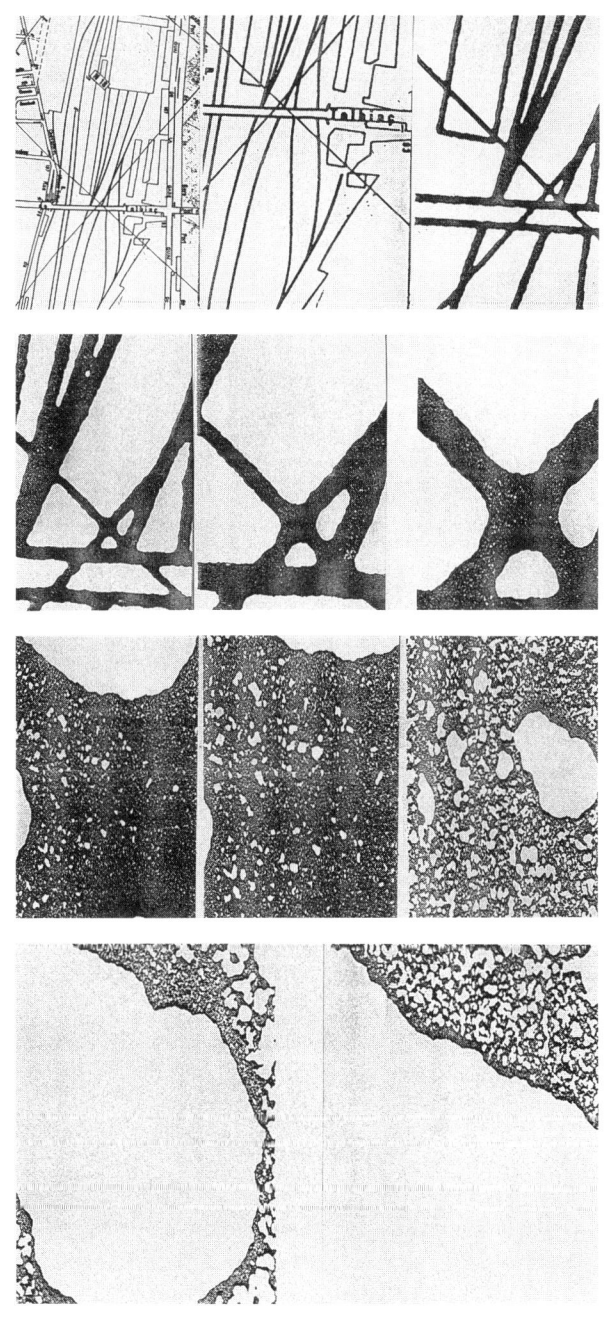

Catherine Ingraham, Michael Freedberg, Peter White, Michael Speaks (at the Chicago Institute for Architecture and Urbanism): "Space-Time Project." This project involved a series of studies of the architectural line. Here a map-line from a Paris city map is transformed through magnification into landscape, anatomical image, porous material, edge condition.

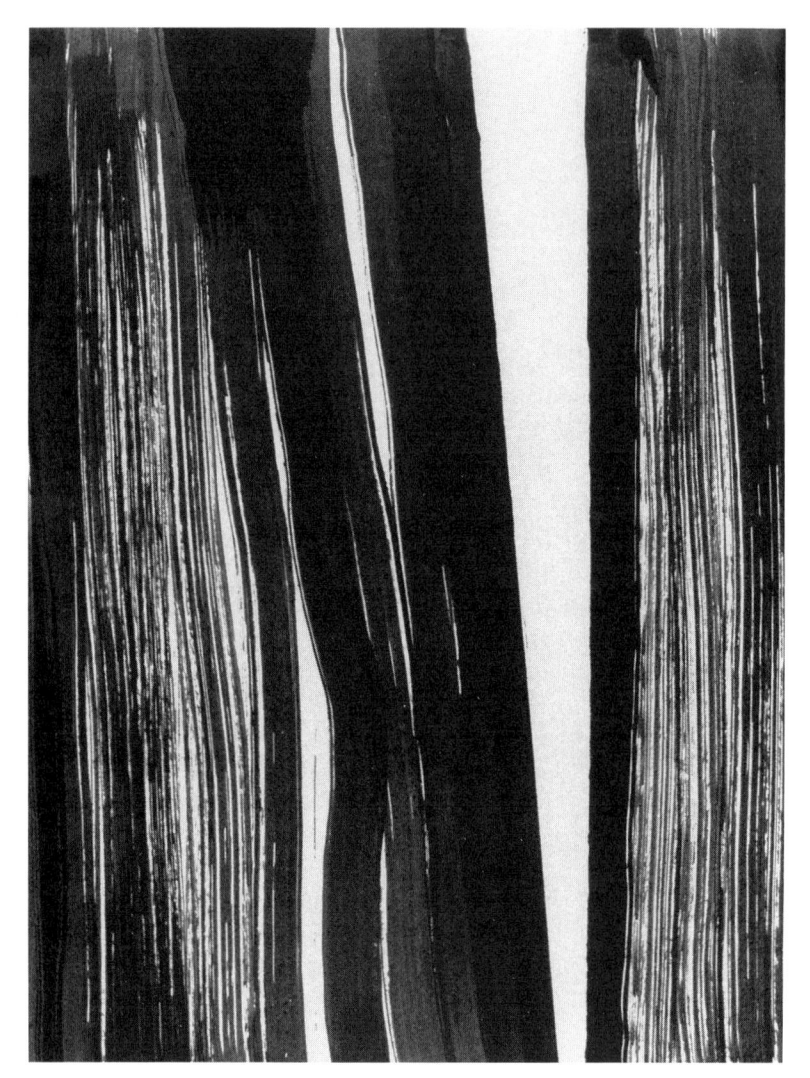

Barnett Newman: Untitled 1946.

For Husserl, the pure geometrical ideality is "released from all sensible or imaginative intuitiveness." The imagination is responsible for the "pure morphological type," and it "can transform sensible shapes only into other sensible shapes." Once pure geometry becomes possible, according to Husserl, it is "accessible only to the understanding," to what Derrida calls "Cartesian intellectualism." Pure geometry is a philosophical act. As Derrida goes on to investigate, the difference between morphological ideality (the ideality already at work in the imperfect geometries of the world) and exact ideality (geometry) is that the latter broke away from its moorings in the world of description (its world of geometrical evidence).[12]

As Derrida argues in his critique of Husserl, the transcendentality of an ideal object is due not to a phenomenological condition, but to the determining frame of the "gemometrico-mathematical horizon."[13] To ask the question of the line within the question of geometry, then, is to immediately enter the linear apparatus—the horizon of linearity—that permits the question in the first place. How, then, can we disentangle ourselves from this net where the line always recaptures us at the moment we begin to unravel it?

Some time ago, I found myself taken with a curious resonance between a series of texts by Le Corbusier, Claude Levi-Strauss, and Jacques Derrida.[14] This resonance had to do with what I called the "burdens of linearity": the way in which philosophical and architectural discussions of lines get mixed up with discussions of beasts of burden (specifically donkeys and mules). This "mixing up" of apparently incongruous lines of discussion may provide a strategy for catching the line as it moves, or transforms itself, from one field of registration to another. I am suggesting that one might be able to see the line as it moves, for example, between the map and the plan, or, between the architectural landscape of the house and the linguistic landscape of the text.[15] Dislodging linear constructs from their proper place becomes the methodological puzzle of this essay: the problem of how to catch the line as its changes its disguise from a mathematical/geometric function, for example, to a written inscrip-

---

12. Husserl, *Origin of Geometry*, 124–135.
13. Husserl, *Origin of Geometry*, 53–54. As Derrida remarks, "all the questions about the possibility or impossibility of maintaining Husserl's demands—either as an essentially inaccessible regulative ideal or as a methodological rule and actual technique . . . are they not asked precisely within this unity of the geometrico-mathematical horizon in general, within the open unity of a science? And it is within the horizon that Husserl here questions that the preoccupation with decidability belongs . . . This whole debate is only understandable within something like *the* geometrical or mathematical science, whose unit is still *to come* on the basis of what is announced in its origins the objective thematic field of mathematics must already be constituted in its mathematical sense, in order for the values of consequence and inconsistency to be rendered problematic." (Derrida's italics).
14. See Catherine Ingraham, "The Burdens of Linearity," delivered in a Fall 1988 theory conference held at the Chicago Institute of Architecture and Urbanism, Chicago, Illinois. (Conference proceedings pending publication.)
15. The line, in its restless generality, keeps us on the move. It repeatedly confounds the pressing desire for specificity—the consideration of specific fields, specific apparatuses, specific histories. The problem with, say, writing a history of architectural perspective (of which there are already a number of examples) is that the line itself always escapes scrutiny. A similar difficulty would arise if one were to undertake an examination of a particular field of lines, say, in a map, plan or drawing, where the "image" presented has already overtaken the linear functions that made it possible in the first place.

tion, or from a "line of sight" of a viewing subject to a "line of identity" of the psychoanalytic subject.

The consequence of mixing up the lines of architecture with, say, the lines of philosophy and/or a discourse on animals is that the line as path (animal path or architectural wall) must be considered in relation to the line as ideal path (pure dimensionless marking). In this juxtaposition it is evident that the power of linearity—a system of lines following the most efficient path, the most ideal state of passage, from one point to another—is related to the complex resistance of an ideal system to its fallen state; for example, the resistance of geometry to animality, impropriety, disease, and contamination. One might discuss this resistance (as I do in the "Burdens" essay) as the resistance of the line to its own inevitable dimensionality, its own thickness and fleshiness. When Le Corbusier, for example, opposes the line to the forces of dispersal—"bestiality" or "irrationality"—he gets caught in the very accusations that the line was supposed to level at the wayward architecture of the past.[16] The linearity he invokes as a defence against architectural barbarities is itself continuously transmogrified into a barbarism.

In a different way, the line attempts to control what Michel Foucault calls the "matrices of power", what Gilles Deleuze and Felix Guattari call "nomadic space"[17], what others call "vector networks" or "wavy lines" or "indirect paths."[18] Here, too, the resistance is one of an ideal system to its inevitable fate in the world. Historically, philosophy and metaphysics have contended with this resistance as a problem of the continuity between mind, spirit, and world. Philosophy habitually asks how we can think the ideal and simultaneously account for our imperfect actions in the world. Thus philosophy begins the division between the faculties—imagination/understanding and intellect/sensibility. We are used to thinking that the real, the everyday, is a falling away from the ideal—the pure geometry, the pure idea. In his paradigmatic critique of writing, Derrida suggests that the very practices that seem farthest fallen are those

16. See my discussion of *The City of Tomorrow* in "The Burdens of Linearity."
17. In Deleuze and Guattari's discussion of "nomadic space" in *Nomadology: The War Machine* the "nomadic trajectory," which "distributes people (or animals) in an open space," is opposed to the "sedentary road," which parcels out "a closed space." Sedentary space is "striated, by walls, enclosures and roads between enclosures, while nomad space is smooth marked only by 'traits' that are effaced and displaced with the trajectory." See: Gilles Deleuze and Felix Guatteri, *Nomadology: The War Machine* (New York: Semiotext(e), 1986), especially 50–51.
18. I am referring to Michel Foucault. It important to note that I want to avoid any hint of the "organic" in this argument. The non-linear is neither the curved, the animalistic, the intuitive, nor the humanistic. The non-linear is the plural.

that instruct us most in the operation of the ideal. "The constitution of the ideal," he remarks, "must . . . pass through the written signifier."[19] The line, as it writes itself everywhere in the world—and perhaps most pointedly (recalling Le Corbusier) in the inarticulate drifting of the animal that carves, through "mindless" routine, a path in the ground—points to the always already failed linearity of the pure geometric line. "The enigmatic model of the *line*," Derrida goes on to say, "is thus the very thing that philosophy could not see when it had its eyes open on the interior of its own history. This night begins to lighten a little at the moment when linearity—which is not loss or absence but the repression of pluri-dimensional symbolic thought—relaxes its oppression because it begins to sterilize the technical and scientific economy that it has long favored."[20] In other words, this "technical and scientific economy" begins to reveal itself as more than merely technical and scientific when the line increases its hold on it, asserting itself as the self-evident path toward clarity, rationality, harmony with nature, and so forth. The slippage of the line's power is inaugurated when one discovers there is no linear path through the line itself.

Architecture has maintained its dedication to linearity in the face of what seems like astounding counter-evidence: the drift and turbulence of forces that can barely be resolved and dissimulated into the vertical striation of space shaped by the column; the tenuousness of graphite on paper or ink on mylar; the loss of resolution in repetition and reproduction; the interior mess of the wall; the extreme materiality and dimensionality—and, in this, the loss of control—of everything architectural. Architecture has, without question, seen linearity as a way of upholding proprieties belonging so completely to its history that it is hard to imagine what architecture would be apart from them. From the geometric propriety allowing us to draw straight lines, other proprieties emerge: the proper nature of materials and universal forces, the proper relationship of the building to the ground, the proper scale and structure of a building. And while the details of this history have changed, the formation of the technical and scientific vocabulary the "line has favored" begins with the very idea of built form.

Let me take one very rich, even mythical, account of the intersection of the linear economy with a built form: Leon Battista Alberti's remarks on the architectural wall in *On The Art of Building in Ten*

---

19. Derrida, *Of Grammatology*, 88.
20. Derrida, *Of Grammatology*, 87.
21. Leon Battista Alberti, *On the Art of Building in Ten Books*, trans. Joseph Rykwert, Neil Leach, Robert Tavernor (Cambridge: MIT Press, 1988).

Books.²¹ I say "mythical" because the burden Alberti's wall must bear—as figure, structure, metaphor—is of mythic proportions. One might keep in mind that the wall is represented in the architectural plan as a double line and is, therefore, a path.

As is well known, Alberti's theory of architecture pivots around what Joseph Rykwert translates as *compartition* and *concinnitas*. Both of these are cosmological conceptions, certainly Platonic in some form, having to do with the relationship of parts to the whole. For Alberti, all the pieces of an architectural composition must fit together and achieve a sense of completion that then produces the harmony between the parts "in appearance." Here, Alberti resorts to the metaphor of the body as a system where all the parts are held together by being filled in. His concept of compartition applies not only to individual building parts, but to the composition of a wall, a house, a city, a column: the wall is to its parts as the house is to the wall, as the city is to the house. The interrelatedness of these parts is paradigmatically organized through the wall as infill and through its composition as skin and bones.

The wall is the dominant anatomical figure in Alberti's theory of architecture. It is part of the material of architecture, according to Alberti, not the act of conceptualization. Conceptually, architecture begins with the *lineamenta*, the outline of the architectural project in the mind.²² The word *lineamenta* does not refer to the drawing of the ground plan or, indeed, any material drawing whatsoever. It refers to the act of conceptualizing a building. As Alberti describes it:

> The whole matter of building is composed of lineaments and structure. All the intent and purpose of lineaments lies in finding the correct, infallible way of joining and fitting together those lines and angles which define and enclose the structures of the building . . . the whole form and appearance of the building may depend on the lineaments alone. Nor do lineaments have anything to do with material, but they are of such a nature that we may recognize the same lineaments in several different buildings that share one and the same form . . . It is quite possible to project whole forms in the mind without any recourse to the material, by designating and determining a fixed orientation and conjunction for the var-

---

22. As Rkywert comments in the Glossary to Alberti's text: "*lineamenta* has been translated variously as *disegni* (Bartoli), meaning drawings and designs; *Risse* (Theuer); 'form' (Panofsky), *Idea*; and by Krautheimer as 'definitions.' 'plan,' and 'schematic outlines'...We have translated it therefore as 'lineaments' for the most part, which encompasses 'lines,' 'linear characteristics,' and so, by implication, design." Alberti, *Ten Books*, 422-423.

The Babylonian World Map on a Cunciform Tablet, ca. 500. BC (British Museum).

ious lines and angles. Since that is the case, let lineaments be the precise and correct outline, conceived in the mind, made up of lines and angles, and perfected in the learned intellect and imagination.[23]

The "joining and fitting together" of lines in the geometric imagination yielding the building outline is outside the material, or bodily, play of parts. The question is how these lineaments can be

23. Alberti, *Ten Books*, 7.

"out of play" in the materiality they engender. There are a number of answers, not least the resurrection of the traditional opposition between ideas and things, conceptuality and physicality; or once again, the division of the mind into separate faculties. But the classical division between the imagination and the intellect gave way, in the twentieth century, to a different model—mainly the Freudian model, where the mind is no longer described as possessing discrete capabilities but, rather, conscious and unconscious levels. The unconscious mind is made up of the residue that the conscious mind finds too dangerous, or too enigmatic, to use. Without performing a simplistic psychoanalytic evaluation of Alberti's text, I want to invoke the Freudian model to suggest that Alberti's lineaments are always already the wall, perhaps one might say the wall as it dreams of itself in the orthogonal drawing. The line, in architecture, is never without the dimensionality and interiority of the wall, even as it proposes to outline an idea. One way this relationship makes itself known in Alberti is the manner in which the lineaments—as a conceptual conceit materially elaborated as the wall—are implicitly marshalled against the catastrophes architecture faces in the world. A short list of the catastrophes Alberti imagines include plague, pollution, floods, bloat, bile, insect bites, monsters, crippling, drought, parasites, chilling darkness, and bad luck, not to mention the more architecturally direct cataclysms of crumbling and collapse. The reduced wall of the line—and its defensive posture—is perhaps not so surprising since the prerequisite of all architecture is that it be present and "stand up." Like the Ptolemaic universe, in which the anomalistic and eccentric paths of the planets were domesticated through elaborate equations that strained against the system, architecture lives with the sense that uprightness—the presence and visibility of form—is a condition won only by keeping to the line.[24]

The ethnologist Robert Ferris Thompson has something interesting to say about the power of "uprightness" that the line enacts through its material power.[25] Speaking about linearity as it figures in what he calls the "artistic criticism" of sub-Sahara Africa, Thompson notes that this criticism uses a sophisticated lexicon of the line to judge the degree of "visibility" in African figurative sculpture. "Visibility," Thompson remarks, "refers to both clarity of

---

24. For a very interesting discussion of "uprighting" and "(re)uprighting," see Ann Bergren, "Baubo and Helen: Gender in the Irreparable Wound," in this volume.
25. I would like to thank Mark Rakatansky for introducing me to the Farris Thompson's discussion of line in Yoruba culture. See Robert Farris Thompson, "Yoruba Artistic Criticism," *The Traditional Artist in African Societies*, ed. Warren L. d'Azevedo (Bloomington: Indiana University Press, 1989), 19–61. All citations from these pages unless otherwise indicated.

Jonathan Borofsky, Untitled.

form and clarity of line." Clarity of line refers to an array of artistic performances that include incising, grooving, and "lining" the eyes, mouth, fingers, ears, and toes of the sculpture. The eye of the face is "opened" by lining it—giving it an outer and inner lining. "Linear connoisseurship" in Yoruba culture is linked with the ritual of cicatrization—the actual cutting of the face to produce ornamental scars. "Since antiquity, Yoruba have adorned their cheeks with lines," Thompson remarks. "They associate lines with civilization. 'This country has become civilized' literally means in Yoruba 'This earth has lines upon its face.'" The same verb that refers to marking the face with lines also refers to clearing the bush and establishing civilization, that is, the uprighting of culture. "The basic verb to cicatrize (la)," Thompson goes on, "has multiple associations with the imposing of human pattern upon the disorder of nature: chunks of wood, the human face, and the forest are all 'opened,' like the human eye, allowing the inner quality of the substance to shine forth."

This passage articulates rather pointedly how linearity brings with it the mythical power of opening, grooving, and incising, that gives "civilized life"—form, shape, visibility, and stature—to land, art, and the human face. One might also say that ethnology itself opens a culture to its investigation through the line of writing. It excavates and brings a culture into alignment with its own (ethnocentric) ideas through lines of writing and paths—that is, "ways back" to ethnic "origins."

Let me take advantage of this "opening" in the mythical structure of linearity to move away from the geometric status of the line toward the problem of the line in writing. Architecture, as a discipline and intellectual practice, is dedicated to the design of inhabitable space. But "design" and "inhabitability" appear as metaphors in other places as well (for example, when we speak of designing a metaphysical system or inhabiting an idea or piece of writing). The thrust of contemporary theory suggests that architecture is as dematerialized, as plural and textual, as the systems of intelligibility—language, science, geometry, graphic, and sculptural arts; it must employ to write itself. But I am interested in the converse proposal: writing (as the paradigmatic operation of language) and philosophy as practices disciplined and instructed by architecture, particularly in matters of "linearity" and inhabitation.

One might read the following comments by Italo Calvino in any number of accounts of writing:

> In devising a story, therefore, the first thing that comes to my mind is an image that for some reason strikes me as charged with meaning, even if I cannot formulate this meaning in discursive or conceptual terms . . . Around each image others come into being, forming a field of analogies, symmetries, confrontations . . . I would say that from the moment of putting black on white, what really matters is the written word, first as a search for an equivalent of the visual image, then as a coherent development . . . Finally, the written word little by little comes to dominate the field.[26]

In this description, the image clusters and then smooths itself out into the line of the text, the written word—its clustering and "field" quality henceforth contained in the linearity of the book. Writing's "domination of the field" occurs because the analogic diffusion of the image is made linear, turned into the path of the written word. This turning of the inarticulate image into a written line is not, however, what it appears. It is neither the reduction of the visual field to the controlled textual field, nor the translation of image into word. Instead, it is the discovery, in the image, of a structure with which writing finds a kind of affinity—mainly, the structure of the

---

26. Italo Calvino, *Six Memos for the Next Millennium* (Cambridge: Harvard University Press, 1988), 89.

line. The image's "linearity" is presented as both its outline and its possibility (as a space-time event that could be mapped in various ways using representative techniques). Writing articulates this linearity explicitly as a line of writing. One might say that writing inhabits, or makes known, the image's linearity. However, one would also have to say that the compression of textuality into a linear path—which is what writing is—does not tame the profusion, the barbarisms and promiscuities, of meaning. Instead, it provisionally encages or houses these barbarisms until they are rereleased through the act of inhabiting the space built by the line (negotiating the line through reading, or negotiating the space of the house).

Writing consists on its surface of spaces and lines that interact with each other according to the combinatory conventions of the twenty-six letters of the alphabet, punctuation marks, diacritical marks, and spacing (margins, movement from left to right, spacing of words, sentences, paragraphs). The graphic character of these marks generally is distinguished from the content or "interior" of writing. Graphic marks are seen as "props" to the act of writing. And yet we are always alert, while writing, to the proper use of its materials—to legibility, proper spelling, the straightness of the line, the preservation of the margin. This attention to the apparatus of writing, in turn, is an attention to the proper inhabitation of the space of writing. The plurality of the text[27] is held in place, propped up, by its linearity, its legibility,[28] its respect for the materiality of

27. In Derrida it is through writing that the operation of discourse and text is announced. In the first section of "The End of the Book and the Beginning of Writing" in *Of Grammatology* he remarks: "By a slow movement whose necessity is hardly perceptible, everything that for at least some twenty centuries tended toward and finally succeeded in being gathered under the name of language is beginning to let itself be transferred to, or at least summarized under, the name of writing ... the concept of writing—no longer indicating a particular, derivative, auxiliary form of language in general ... no longer designating the exterior surface, the insubstantial double of a major signifier, *the signifier of the signifier*—is beginning to go beyond the extension of language. In all senses of the word, writing thus *comprehends* language. Not that the word "writing" has ceased to designate the signifier of the signifier, but it appears, strange as it may seem, that 'signifier of the signifer' no longer defines accidental doubling and fallen secondarity." (Derrida, *Of Grammatology*, 6–26) Further, Derrida remarks in "The Violence of the Letter" in the same volume, that "if a text always gives itself a certain representation of its own roots, those roots live only by that representation, by never touching the soil, so to speak ... a text is never anything but a *system of roots*."
28. One might speak of a typology of reading consisting of a series of known structures—the poetic, narrative, discursive, philosophical, and so forth. Like architectural typologies, these rely on certain conventions related to proper function. Writing arranged according to the linear structure of poetry has difficulty passing itself off as novelistic, although various interesting experiments have been tried along these lines. Typologies of reading are rigid and influence every aspect of written space.

the page and the book. When Derrida speaks of the "end of the book and the beginning of writing" he means to expose the false closure of the book. But as he continuously cautions, we inhabit these shelters even as we expose them. It is precisely the concept of the shelter or space or structure, which subsists behind an unexamined metaphoricalness in philosophy, that must return in the interest of architecture. One might say that the rooms of philosophy—the material structure of writing being one such room—are given their pleasure, their logic, their comfort, their inescapableness, by the formulation of these desires and structures vis-à-vis architecture. From poststructural philosophy we learn that one leaves the "house" only provisionally. But from architecture we learn about the range of possible formulations of inhabitable space; that is, we learn the power of the house. This is, traditionally, a deeply conservative knowledge.[29] Architecture as a discipline, like philosophy, activates its own interior knowledge without reflecting on the apparatus that makes its epistemology cohere in a particular way. In the interior of writing and architecture—which is where theory and philosophy and "life" negotiate their terms—what begins as a material/spatial structure becomes figurative: metonymic or metaphoric.[30] Philosophy and writing employ the "architectural metaphor" as the trace of a material structure, a *presence-structure*, in order to preserve the architectural nature of discourse without attending to its material implications.

As I suggested above, writing in the colloquial sense—as a spatial act—is restricted by conventions of orthography just as architecture is restricted by conventions of orthogonality. To inhabit a piece of writing one enters into its orthographic conventions. The perniciousness of a failed or violated orthography—such as the misspelled word or de-linearized sentence, phrase, and so on—can be felt perhaps most poignantly in Derrida's tampering with the word "difference." The substitution of the "a" for "e" in "differ*a*nce," the

---

29. See Catherine Ingraham, "The Faults of Architecture: Troping the Proper," *Assemblage* 7 (MIT Press:1988) where I discuss the power of the house as the power of "propriety"—moral systems, property systems, and the force of the proper name. Architecture traditionally instructs philosophy in the *proper* forms of inhabitation; architecture is a powerful raconteur of the socially, politically, ideologically proper. When this architectural system of the proper is transgressed, philosophy and culture (patriarchal governance, self-identity, ideological systems, etc.) flounder as severely as the shelter and "home" that this system makes possible. Architecture attempts to keep things in line, in all senses of the word.

30. As Roland Barthes has said, moments of dysfunction are recuperated as tragic or poetic acts, as myths. One might say that the "architectural metaphor" claims the moment of architectural (material) interruption in philosophical discourse as a philosophical myth.

genealogy of that act, the burden it carries in Derrida's entire critique of writing, throws into relief and confusion the workings of an unreflective orthographic government. The "e" inhabits the word difference in a specific way that cannot be changed without consequences. Indeed, it is precisely because orthographic interventions seriously fissure writing that Derrida sets out on the path of differ*a*nce to begin with. We inhabit the space of the word, and the space between words, with as much restriction and latitude as we inhabit rooms in a house.

Writing, in the Derridean sense, is the paradigmatic material structure for the decentralization of language and being. Importantly, it is the colloquial sense of writing—writing that has already fallen from speech because it must be inscribed, writing that strings signifiers together and unfolds in time—that, for Derrida, leverages the whole critique of western metaphysics. Architecture is the paradigmatic material structure for the centering of language and being, "being at home with itself." These structures do not tolerate each other, and yet this intolerance only conceals the disturbing implications of two linear structures that house each other. The difference, competition, and interdependence between these structures takes place, as I have already suggested, at the level of the apparatus they employ in order to inscribe themselves. At the same time that the material apparatus of writing forces itself into the paradigmatic "centering" of architecture, the material apparatus of architecture forces itself into the paradigmatic "decentering" of writing. These two kinds of inscriptionality, where inscriptionality is the necessary but not sufficient condition for their enactment, ignore each other at their peril. As the hidden structural prop—one might recall Aldo Rossi's table of preparation—architecture stages a certain domestic scene in the midst of writing and philosophy. Like the primal scene of psychoanalysis, this is a scene of seduction, the seduction of writing into a linear path so that we may inhabit it.

Finally, we cannot do without some account of the subject in this drama of the line. While many disciplines use orthographic systems—geography, cartography, painting, and so on—only architecture must directly contend with the problem of inhabiting the space of linear geometries. Architecture, therefore, to some degree, must construct the inhabiting subject along geometric lines. To do this, of course, the subject undergoes a certain orthogonal stylization. As the Vitruvian man or Le Corbusier's modulor have shown us, this architecturalizing of the subject often takes the form of inscribing in, or measuring the body against, geometric space. But there are other forms of architecturalizing the subject, notably the Lacanian positioning of the self.

The self, as Jacques Lacan characterizes it, is not a consciousness present to itself. As Lacan's mirror stage theory suggests, the act of intelligence by which a child recognizes his or her image in a mirror, "immediately rebounds... in a series of gestures in which [the child] experiences in play the relation between the movements assumed in the image and the reflected environment, and between the virtual complex and the reality it reduplicates—the child's own body, and the persons and things, around him." Lacan continues:

We have only to understand the mirror stage as an identification, in the full sense that analysis gives to the term: namely, the transformation that takes place in the subject when he assumes an image. [The maturation of the child's formal power is] given to him only as ... an exteriority in which this form is certainly more constituent than constituted, but in which it appears to him above all in a contrasting size that fixes it and in a symmetry that inverts it ... by these two aspects of its appearance, [it] symbolizes the mental permanence of the I, at the same time as it prefigures its alienating destination.[31]

Lacan's theory describes the alienation of the child in and through space. The mirror returns the image of the self to the self as image, as other. The temporal distance signified by the speed of light required to illuminate the image in the mirror (or any reflecting surface) is, in some sense, a paradigmatic distance always subsisting between the self as consciousness and self as other. This distance is, in turn, the paradigmatic distance between the self and the visible world; it shapes the relationship between these two "entities" as a spatial and supplemental one that attempts to gratify the insufficiency of each side.[32]

The spatial and material dynamics of Lacan's theory resurrects the line—of sight, image, inhabitation, writing, architecture—as a line of identity. The mirror is both a narcissistic[33] apparatus for captur-

---

31. Lacan, *Ecrits*, 1–3.
32. Lacan discusses this insufficiency as follows: "The mirror stage is a drama whose internal thrust is precipitated from insufficiency to anticipation—and which manufactures for the subject, caught up in the lure of spatial identification, the succession of phantasies that extends from a fragmented body-image to a form of its totality that I shall call orthopaedic—and lastly, to the assumption of the armour or an alienating identity, which will mark with its rigid structure the subject's entire mental development." (*Ecrits*, 4)
33. The myth of Narcissus recounts how Narcissus sees, falls in love with, and is transfixed by his image in the pool until he dies. The child Narcissus was ravishingly beautiful and therefore courted by other youth. But he was also prideful and scorned admiration. The nymph Echo, doomed to repeat the last words of others, loved Narcissus and was among those spurned by him. Unable to embrace his own image, Narcissus lay beside the pool until he died of starvation. His body metamorphosed into a flower. Narcissus' self-love pivots around the spatial threshold, the mirror-space of self-identity, but the figure of Echo takes up the same theme of reflection in a

ing the self and, simultaneously, an apparatus for the inversion and distancing of the self through reflective imaging. As a psychoanalytic metaphor, the mirror functions as an emblem of the simultaneous formation and alienation of identity. As a spatial apparatus, the mirror institutes the problem of space—and its resultant subject/object confusions—as a fundamental condition for the development of human identity.[34] The architectural force of the mirror resides in its commentary on the structural relationship of subject to object, space to identity. In Lacan's scheme, the young child must be propped up (presumably by an adult) in front of the mirror in order to see its reflection.[35] This "propping up" indicates an apparatus (partially hidden) in Lacan's theory, an apparatus that enables and constitutes the act of looking, and the act of imaging, in a certain way. This propping structure does not itself rebound in any explicit sense; its image, which would also display reversal and symmetry, is subordinated to the image of the child. This structure does not see itself, nor can it be seen, finally, in the constitution of the subject, and yet, without it, the initial engagement with the spatial act of identification is rendered impossible. The spatial distance implicit in the act of imaging and the apparatus of the prop produce an architectural analog for the "orthopaedic" fantasy—the felt totality of the (fragmented) material body.

The architectural scaffolding implied by this identity story is the appearance of architecture in a place from which one's attention has been distracted.[36] Lacan's mirror-space theory of the self depends on the effaced structure of the architectural prop. The arrival at a

different way—through the refracted voice. See: Edward Tripp, *Crowell's Handbook of Classical Mythology* (New York: Thomas Y. Crowell Company, 1970), 389.

34. The grammatological counterpart to the mirror is the space between the signifier and the signified in language. This space, as Derrida describes it, is temporally established: "the order of the signified is never contemporary, is at best the subtly discrepant inverse or parallel—discrepant by the time of a breath—from the order of the signifier. And the sign must be the unity of a heterogeneity, since the signified (sense or thing, noema or reality) is not in itself a signifier . . . The formal essence of the signified is *presence* . . . The 'formal essence' of the sign can only be determined in terms of presence. One cannot get around that response, except by challenging the very form of the question and beginning to think that the sign is that ill-named thing, the only, that escapes the instituting question of philosophy: "what is . . . ?" Derrida, *Of Grammatology*, 18–19.

35. Beatriz Colomina called my attention to this propping apparatus during a conversation about the implication of Lacan's theory for architecture.

36. In "The Faults of Architecture," I suggest that architecture is a discipline of the elsewhere, of distraction. It is only by reenlivening the tropic dimension of architecture without decent limit—the textuality of form or form giving, which is a promiscuous and improper act—that we can begin to surprise architecture in its disciplinary and epistemological claims, to catch it out in places where, properly, it has no right to be.

theory of identity is also an arrival at a certain theory of space, apparatus, body and structure. Here the body is scaffolded and propped in decisive ways by the materiality—the presence, the armature—we attribute to architecture and then built up as different from architecture within this framework. The body is "architected" according to the scale, not of the body in some natural state, but of the body already built in space as image. Or, rather, the body as subject is built only after a spatial and architectural identification has taken place.

The "line" of representation that allows us to position ourselves outside of the objects designed by us or for us is here seen to be already complicated by the scaffolding that props us up before our own image. It is important to reiterate that, according to Lacan, we do not exist as a consciousness, nor does the visible world exist before our encounter with our own alienated image in the mirror. Whether this mirror-stage refers to a literal mirroring of the self or simply the way we must be mirrored to ourselves through the eyes of the "mother"[37]—the prop must always be present before the visible world is opened to us, before we are able to represent it in any way. One might say that the architect tries to supply the insufficiency of the fragmented whole—the self and the body—by sketching the scaffolding as a web to keep us forever propped upright in front of our own image. Or, rather, the architect tries to hold us, using the force of lines, at the moment of the méconnaisance, the mis-recognition that inaugurates our belief in the possibility of space and inhabitation. Necessarily, this condition is a double one and one in which the architect, too, is caught. It is the condition of Narcissus frozen before his image in the pool and the condition of the child who grows up to see (himself/herself) in (architectural) space.

---

37. It is important to remark that the "mother" does not refer to a specific gender (i.e. female) but to the person in whose eyes the child finds an identity reflection. See Jacquelin Rose's remarks in the introduction to Jacques Lacan, *Feminine Sexuality* (New York: W.W. Norton, 1982). "Lacan's account of subjectivity was always developed with reference to the idea of a fiction. Thus, in the 1930s he introduced the concept of the 'mirror stage' (*Ecrits*, 1936), which took the child's mirror image as the model and basis for its future identifications. This image is a fiction because it conceals, or freezes, the infant's lack of motor coordination and the fragmentation of its drives. But it is salutary for the child, since it gives it the first sense of a coherent identity in which it can recognize itself. For Lacan, however, this is already a fantasy—the very image which places the child divides its identity into two. Furthermore, that moment only has meaning in relation to the presence and the look of the mother who guarantees its reality for the child. The mother does not ... mirror the child to itself; she grants an image to the child, which her presence instantly deflects. Holding the child is, therefore, to be understood not only as a containing, but as a process of referring, which fractures the unit it seem to offer." (*Feminine Sexuality*, 30–31.)

ANDREA KAHN

THE INVISIBLE MASK

He's afraid of the way the glass will fall—soon—it will be a spectacle: the fall of a crystal palace. But coming down in total blackout, without one glint of light, only great invisible crashing.—Thomas Pynchon, Gravity's Rainbow

Contemporary architectural culture is preeminently concerned with the visible: architecture as image; the architectural drawing as aesthetic object; the idea in a vital strain of postmodern design that architecture should *look like* architecture; and the tendency to translate theoretical discourse into material constructions illustrate this concern. The relationship of politics to architecture is also considered in visual terms; particular buildings, forms, or styles are seen as potent representations of ruling authority or ideology. Architecture's capacity for explicit political symbolization does not, however, describe the full scope of its power, nor is its power limited to the spatial manifestation of institutional programs (rules and agendas) in physical form. Rather, the political nature of architecture is rooted more deeply in architecture as enclosure and in the manner in which enclosure is perceived.

In simple terms, to enclose is to surround or mark off with a fence, to delineate a particular space within a larger field. By transforming part of a general spatial domain into a specific site for a particular use (public or private), architecture divides, organizes and manages. It orders physical movement and proscribes perception. Architecture is the disciplinization of space, and, by virtue of its capacity to regulate action, exerts control and constitutes a form of power.

The deployment of this power does not depend upon the apparent image of architecture, or upon what it expresses either directly, or by association. It is not allied to form or iconography, but to perception. According to Walter Benjamin, architecture provides an example of an art "the reception of which is consummated by a collectivity in a state of distraction." Benjamin saw in this mode of perception art's potential to politically effect an essentially absent-minded public. In his words, it allowed for a "covert control."[1]

Benjamin's observation renders suspect a preoccupation with the strictly visible in architecture. His remarks also expand the concept of function beyond the program delineating particular actions or rituals like dwelling, working, and studying. The covert power noted by Benjamin exists apart from program, functions independent of specific political agendas (fascist, democratic, etc.), and is distinct from representational formulae that invite conscious focus. It is embodied, instead, in the presentational elements of architecture, each of which constitutes an apparatus of control: walls erect barriers to free movement; windows, in framing given views, determine the scope of vision; thresholds tell us where to go.

The architectural object is not taken in with rapt attention devoted to painting or sculpture. Rather, it is absorbed incidentally. Like the ubiquitous landscape unfolding beyond the windshield of a car, simultaneously seen and not seen by a driver intent upon "watching the road," the politically performatory aspects of architecture slip by or slip into one's consciousness almost unnoticed. Receiving something in a state of distraction implies an indirect act of looking—beyond, through, or past the immediate object. Although not expressly stated in Benjamin's text, to look past is at once to see past—in the sense of overlooking or dismissing. This oversight of architecture's political effects allows for unwitting acceptance of, or submission to, a controlling power hidden or enclosed within the readily seen.

To discern this power one must attend to the invisible in architecture. How is its covert operation effected and what does it impress upon a viewer or user?

THE PALACE: ELISIONS

The design of the building should be as original as its object.
—W. Bridges Adam

The covert functions or tacit politic (power relations) of architecture are illustrated by Joseph Paxton's Crystal Palace. By shedding all

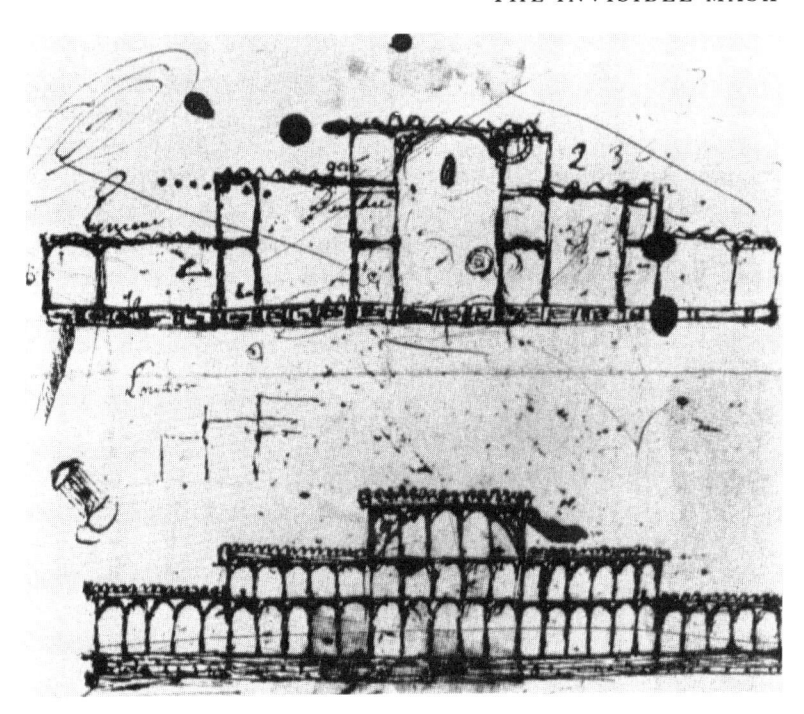

Joseph Paxton's first sketch for the Crystal Palace, 1850.

remnants of an opaque building skin, it did not obscure, obstruct, or enclose in a typical architectural sense. The Crystal Palace was built in Hyde Park, London to house the first International Great Exhibition of 1851. This monument to consumer capitalism was the product of England's highly developed industry and, according to Siegfried Giedion, was "an application of the most simple and rational system of manufacturing—serial production."[2] A slow start on the part of the Exhibitions Building Committee, opposition to a permanent structure in the park, concern for existing trees, and the impossibility of completing the committee's own proposal in time for the event contributed to the consideration of Paxton's late competition entry. Though the structure was suited to its park site, quickly designed, and easily assembled (and disassembled), the Building Committee—particularly engineers who sustained substantial doubts about reliance on iron and glass as the sole materials for such a large structure—still resisted Paxton's building. By leaking his design to the press, Paxton undercut the commission's authority and captivated public interest for his project. By mid July, the Royal Commission had rejected the building committee's proposal in favor of Paxton's plan.

The Crystal Palace marked architecture's entry into an era of increased industrial power, newly developing international economies, and technological advances in materials and methods of construction. According to Georg Kohlmaier, the building accommodated 17,000 exhibitors, held over 1 million items, and boasted 6 million visitors. It was 1848 feet long and 408 feet wide and required 900,000 square feet of glazing and over 6,500 iron structural columns, pillars, and beams, all mass-produced in standardized dimensions. The method of fabrication allowed for both on- and off-site production in a highly coordinated process that kept costs to a minimum. (The 1851 International Exhibition actually turned a profit.)[3]

The modern materials and construction techniques of Paxton's project resulted in the ideal exhibition hall. The objects on display were framed by the building's structural system and enhanced by the light admitted through its transparent skin. As a monumental vitrine for commodities, the Crystal Palace successfully fulfilled the prophetically modern criteria suggested to the Building Committee by W. Bridges Adam who, in calling for a design "as original as its object" elaborated,

It should not be suggestive of the ideas of a pyramid, a temple or a palace; for it will not be a tomb, a place of public worship, nor a mansion of royalty. The object should determine the design. That is to say, the design should be altogether subordinate to the uses of the building, and should be of the kind that would express them, or at least harmonize with them.[4]

Compared with Victorian revivalist architecture, the Crystal Palace offered a potential escape from the uncomfortable tyranny of past styles. It did, however, have programmatic and material precedents in the 19th century, particularly the commercial arcades, which from the early 1800s adopted ever more sophisticated ferro-vitreous roofing systems. These were dependent upon advances in technology that also produced larger shop windows permitting the exhibit of wares even after business hours. The glass-enclosed pedestrian streets provided a protected environment for the flaneur or consumer. In their characteristically interstitial urban sites they enticed the masses with glimpses of luxury goods ultimately intended for the upper class. The arcades institutionalized "shopping" as opposed to buying, where the act of looking, fostered by and fueling desire, was as important as actually purchasing items.[5]

Where the arcade was reliant structurally upon existing masonry urban fabric and programmatically upon existing retail shops, the Crystal Palace was a freestanding structure housing an independent and temporary trade enterprise. Its location in Hyde Park distinguished it from the architecture of the city and allied it to a tradition of garden structures. Paxton designed the largest glass-and-iron building to date, drawing materially and typologically on orangeries

Construction Work, the Crystal Palace, January, 1851. Woodcut.

and horticultural glass houses. Commissioned by and for the pleasure of the landed nobility, such buildings operated as microclimates, machines to protect the works of nature from her own hostile elements. Enclosed plants became "specialty items" displayed like the specialty items of industry in the arcades, their growth enhanced—forced—by the solar properties of glass.

Conflating the mechanistic quality of the orangery with the commercial program of the arcade, the Crystal Palace superimposed the house of nature and the house of trade. Exhibiting industrial wares in the place of horticultural specimens, the Palace signalled the rising dominance of industrial forces over the natural environment. Its peculiar mechanistic novelty and its artificial materials stripped the Palace of visibly representational architectural iconography; the vistas of the park compensated for the structure's lack of a conventional architectural image. From the exterior, the structural frame doubled as viewing frame, guiding the eye toward the contents of the hall and highlighting the already objectified condition of the commodity. Like the broad sidewalks of Haussmann's Paris boulevards, the Palace created a space of

Palm Garden City of Frankfurt, 1869–71. Engraving of interior view.

public spectacle where the visitors themselves were on display, as consumable as the products they came to see if not actually procure.[6] On the interior, the products of industry, basking in the purity of nature's sunlight, were viewed in a space shared by the work of nature (the main transept enclosed a stand of mature elms) suggesting a benevolent relationship between culture and nature and belying the co-option of the landscape to enhance the image of industry. The building's transparent surface, meanwhile, offered constant panoramas of Hyde Park. The architecture of the Crystal Palace allied the act of shopping with the act of observing nature, not to commodify nature but to naturalize commodification.

The program, conception, and construction of the exhibition building were intimately bound up with industrialization, and the Palace's effect on the viewer is similar to that of the picturesque landscape. As opposed to the rationalized French formal garden, the English country garden involved a manipulation of nature so "natural" as to escape notice. Critical evaluations of the picturesque point to the politics underlying this design strategy. To paraphrase Steven Daniels, there are two sensibilities at play in the picturesque, one

THE INVISIBLE MASK

Royal Botanical Garden, Kew, London, 1844-48. Engraving of Palm House and Victoria Regia House.

articulating a critique of social and economic issues through landscape, the other using landscape to obscure these same issues.[7] In the picturesque landscape what is taken as natural is in fact quite the opposite: cultivated, worked, schemed.

The picturesque landscape depends upon a design strategy geared toward making the act of design—as well as its underlying politics—invisible. Similarly, the Crystal Palace obscured even as it revealed. The act of "seeing through" the iron and glass structure out to the park or in toward the elm trees concealed a simultaneous act of "seeing past" industry's transformation of nature into a marketing device. As Benjamin notes:

> The world exhibitions build up the universe of commodities ... Fashion prescribes the ritual according to which the commodity fetish wishes to be worshipped; Grandville extends fashion's claims both to the objects of everyday use and to the cosmos. By pursing it to its extremes he discloses its nature. This resides in a conflict with the organic. It couples the living body to the inorganic world.[8]

The Crystal Palace exemplified architecture's capacity to embody such a conflicted coupling and foster free market economics. Its legacy is obvious in projects like Cesar Pelli's Wintergarden design for Battery Park City in lower Manhattan. A large glass-enclosed space provides the major public amenity amidst a group of private office buildings; the free movement through the Wintergarden contrasts the highly secured thresholds of the accompanying corporate towers. Lined with expensive specialty shops and filled with palm trees specially bred to survive under New York City lighting conditions, this mall cum garden opens to vistas of the Hudson River. It links the financial hub of the city to nature—physically and metaphorically—and so borrows directly from the marketing strategy of the Crystal Palace.

The Palace elided nature and industry. According to Marshall Berman, contemporary accounts of Paxton's building reveal

a structure with gentle flowing lines and graceful curves, light almost to the point of weightlessness, looking as if it could float at any instant into the sky. Its color alternates between the color of the sky through the transparent glass, which covers most of the building's volume, and the sky blue of its narrow iron beams; this combination drenches us in a dazzling radiance, catching the sunlight from the sky and the water, shimmering dynamically. Visually, the building feels like a late Turner painting; it particularly suggests Turner's *Rain, Steam and Speed* (1844) fusing nature and industry in a vividly chromatic and dynamic ambiance.[9]

It glazed over the boundary between interior and exterior, denying the solidity and as such the discernible closure of the building and it also obscured disciplinary distinctions. In Paxton's own words:

No single feature, but the structure as a whole, would form a peculiar novelty of mechanical science; and, when we consider the manner of supporting a vast glass roof covering twenty-one acres on the most secure and scientific principles, and filling in a structure of such magnitude with glass, Mr. Paxton ventures to think that such a plan would meet with almost universal approval of the British public, whilst it would be unrivalled in the world.[10]

Unlike the greenhouses and arcades preceding it, the Crystal Palace engendered a moment of self-questioning for architecture. Physically, architecture builds distinctions between here and there; spatially it defines limits by erecting enclosures and visible barriers. Epistemologically, as well, architecture delimits itself from other fields of thought and action; acceptable ideas and practices are enclosed and unacceptable ones foreclosed by invisible barriers shaping the discipline.

THE INVISIBLE MASK

The Crystal Palace posed visible and invisible threats to architecture: materially, its window-wall did not provide a traditional sense of physical closure and its constantly fluctuating surface denied a certain solidity and permanence previously associated with architectural form; conceptually, disciplinary closure was jeopardized because the mode of construction fused engineering and architectural practices. The unstable images flickering on its glazed surface suggest a prescient visual metaphor for the destabilizing effect of modern theory and polemics on traditional conceptions of architecture.

The building's potential impact on architecture as discipline and on conventional architectural production did not go unheeded by contemporaries. According to Lothar Bucher, "In contemplating the first great building which was not of solid masonry construction spectators were not slow to realize that here the standards by which architecture had hitherto been judged no longer held good."[11]

The Palace failed to fit neatly into established typological or disciplinary categories, and historical accounts reflect its uncertain status. In Pevsner's *Pioneers of Modern Design* of 1936 the Crystal Palace is considered as much a feat of engineering as a work of architecture and discussion of the building is set among "testimonies on iron . . . stimulated by structures which were not architecture with a capital A."[12] A year later, in the catalogue introduction to the 1937 MoMA show "Modern Architecture in England," Henry-Russell Hitchcock would describe Paxton's project as a "direct ancestor of modern architecture . . . often hailed with pardonable exaggeration as the first modern building."[13]

The Crystal Palace fostered commodification via remarkable mastery of modern capitalist ideals, but its inclusion in the canon as 'the first modern building' arose from its technology and materials, not its program. Of these, its extensive glazed surface was the most conspicuous—literally and metaphorically.

MATERIAL ILLUSIONS

The whole being covered in with glass, renders the building light, airy and suitable—Joseph Paxton

In "Transparency: Literal and Phenomenal" Colin Rowe and Robert Slutsky explore the notion of transparency, a concept (as they point out in their introduction) "richly loaded" with meaning.[14] Drawing on the writings of Gyory Kepes, the authors distinguish between literal transparency as a function of material attributes and transparency as a phenomenon perceived through spatial organiza-

Richard Estes, *Railway Station, Venice*, 1975. Painting.

The Eiffel Tower in Jacques Tati's *Playtime*. Film still.

Richard Estes, *Alitalia*, 1973. Painting.

tion, the former having the physical quality of being perfectly clear and the latter being "clearly ambiguous." While the qualities of physically transparent materials are not central to the argument, they too pose certain ambiguities. Clear glass is on first sight neutral, dismissive. On closer inspection, however, it reveals "a simultaneous perception of different spatial locations" where space recedes and "fluctuates in a continuous activity," qualities of phenomenal transparency described by Kepes and essential to Rowe and Slutsky's distinction.

Transparent glass, in contrast to the constancy of reflective (mirror) glass exhibits a variety of perceivable states. Mirror replaces the physical density of solid building materials with the perceptual opacity of surface images; it does not reveal its interior nor do its reflections generate spatial ambiguity. The images appropriated from surrounding forms to constitute such an architectural skin may change as the atmosphere changes, but their location is always the outer layer of a surface plane. The depth one reads in a mirror reflection is the depth of the space in front of it, not a phenomenal depth created by the glazed surface itself. Clear glass, on the other hand, can disappear, become invisible, and simultaneously be the locus of activity; the reflections in a Richard Estes painting, for example create complex dimensional spaces trapped by and at once transgressing the physical limits of the surface. The view through and beyond the clear glass is inseparable from and informed by the images reflected upon it.

Whether the skin of the Crystal Palace dematerialized matters less than that under any lighting condition its glazed surface served materialistic ends. When transparent, the structure offered immediate views both inside and out. When reflective, the extensive surface planes increased the already massive volume of display space, redoubling the spectacle in a virtual image caught and extended by the glazed skin.

The architecture of the Palace was unclothed and the character as well as the function of its nudity depended upon its alternatively reflective and transparent state. Reflections are like strippers, playing with the act of veiling and unveiling to titillate with a body sometimes covered, sometimes bare. Inciting desire, reflections transform the viewer into the voyeur whose eye has the power of appropriation without purchase. On its interior, the Palace's reflective surface promoted the voyeuristic gaze attendant to shopping, allowing goods and people to be espied indirectly. On the exterior, reflections afforded a redoubled vision of the surrounding park, diminishing the presence of the building in its midst. By contrast, transparent glass is unselfconscious, naked, pure; it allowed the Palace to be allied with a legitimate morality—permissive without being promiscuous, natural. From the park, the glass skin created the image of an "non-exclusive" interior realm, while from inside it transformed Hyde Park into a scenographic backdrop enhancing the display of commercial wares.

A potent and critical illustration of glass's ambiguity appears in Jacques Tati's *Playtime*. The film follows a group of American tourists on a visit to Paris that entails a day amidst sleek glass and steel skyscrapers in "Tativille," an environment that prefigures La Defense. Images of Paris (the Louvre, Montmartre, the Eiffel Tower, etc.) are reflected in the plate glass facades of these modern buildings. Tati's carefully framed shots through curtain walls sometimes reflective, sometimes clear, lend glass an almost oppressive quality. It is at once disorienting (one character is unable to differentiate between the reflection and the actual location of a wall), alienating (one can see but not reach a destination), deceiving (a doorman opening and closing a nonexistent plate glass door by its brass handle), and voyeuristic (the sanctity of private home life is espied from the street through plate-glass walls). The film is a portrait of a material that in spite of and through its transparency empowers and disempowers by effecting lines of sight.

THE IDEAL OF TRANSPARENCY

"... *a person who daily sets his eyes on the splendors of glass cannot do wicked deeds.*"—Paul Scheerbart

Glass, which casts no visible shadows, has long been associated in architecture with utopian visions. In the early 1800s Fourier proposed glass enclosed galleries for his phalansteries, whose "warmth and security, exoticism and almost stifling excitement... would also stimulate its inhabitants to experiment endlessly in the forms of sensual pleasure, thus bringing about the Nouveau monde amoureux."[15] Following the success of the Crystal Palace, Paxton proposed a Crystal Way for London, a heated ring-road complete with underground rail lines, an unbuilt urban ideal that spawned other similar proposals, including a commercial Crystal Way shopping loop bordering a central park described by Ebenezer Howard in his 1898 *Garden Cities of Tomorrow*. Paul Scheerbart in his "Glass Manifesto" of 1914 called for the replacement of brick and masonry architecture, claiming that to "raise culture to a higher level" would "be possible only if we remove the enclosed quality from the spaces within which we live. This can be done only through the introduction of glass architecture."[16]

The ascription of architectural meaning is arbitrary, yet, through repeated use, materials and forms acquire conventional connotations. Traditionally, transparency has been allied to social agendas associated with positive ends. No matter how benevolently motivated, however, such agendas are predicated upon programs of power. If architects express these programs uncritically and viewers absorb them without question, conventional "meaning" assumes an invisible, covert power to obscure alternative readings.

For modern architects in general, eschewal of tradition styles and their allied rhetorical forms heightened the symbolic potential of materials. For Scheerbart and the other architects of the Glass Chain (a group assembled around Bruno Taut in 1919, including Gropius, Scharoun, Finsterlin, and Behne) in particular, glass represented a collective purity; its transparent quality had both politically and morally symbolized "cosmic liberation."[17]

The roots of such thinking can be traced to the Enlightenment. Rousseau believed that crystal was the only innocent stone. Transparency was the opposite of alienation—the unveiling of truth, goodness free from the distorted visions of other men. Similarly, the clear glass skin of Paxton's Palace "unveiled" the building's structural system to the eye; the Palace's "truth" was revealed in a book containing all the construction documents and detail drawings from the building process. As Leiberman notes of this text "We are as far as we can be from the jealously guarded knowledge of medieval masons; the modern age was to replace secret techniques with building methods as publicly known and as universally reproducible as scientific experiment."[18]

Joseph Paxton, Crystal Palace, Sydenham, 1852–54.

"The possibilities dormant in modern industrial civilization have never since, to my knowledge, been so clearly expressed" writes Giedion, playing on the both the literal and figurative senses of "clearly" to praise the success of the Palace.[19] Yet, like its physical counterpart, metaphorical clarity also entails ambiguity. Rousseau's wish for transparency—stemming from a desire to disclose his true self—contains the very threat of falsity it tries to overcome. Transparency that reveals the true self at once renders it invisible, open to replacement by false appearance. As Jean Starobinski has written regarding Rousseau, the ideal of transparency as pure lucidity (moral or otherwise) entails a paradox, "In an extreme sense, transparency is equivalent to perfect invisibility. Others see me as different from what I am, hence they do not see me. I am invisible to them."[20] Thus, the desire to disclose truth can ultimately lead to its erasure.

Transparency to the point of invisibility contains the danger of being co-opted by the vision of others. In the myth of the ring of Gyges (a myth about transparency and power—seeing and being seen) the wearer of the ring can become invisible, thereby acquiring the authority of the king, the all-seeing overseer who escapes the gaze of others. For Rousseau, this also suggested omnipotence:

"Had I been invisible and powerful like God, I would also have been good and benevolent ... Had I possessed the ring of Gyges, it would have made me independent of men and made them dependent upon me. I have often wondered, in my castles in the air, how I would have used this ring."[21]

"Invisibility" as Starobinski remarked after citing the above passage, "converts the nullity of being into unlimited power."

The Crystal Palace seemingly does away with material architectural distractions as compared, for example, to the buildings of the Columbian Exposition (Chicago, 1893) where new technology dressed up in old plaster-of-paris clothes. By virtue of the glass and iron structure, one sees and sees past the Crystal Palace at the same time. The degree of control is heightened by being rendered invisible.

From Palace to Prison

Lucid transparency was very much to his taste, as is evident from his recollection of a French Fairy Tale in which the Heroine had been imprisoned in a palace of solid glass: 'of this archetype the Panopticon was as near a similitude as the limited power of human art could admit.
—Robin Evans on Jeremy Bentham

Joseph Paxton's Crystal Palace bears a curious similarity to Jeremy Bentham's Penitentiary Panopticon. The former is linear and the latter centrally organized; the two programs are decidedly opposite—the pleasures of consumption against the pains of incarceration (although Bentham was most intrigued with the use of both pain and pleasure in achieving his reforms); in terms of explicit imagery and primary materials, their affiliation also seems improbable. Yet, as Evans has written, the essential order of the prison, like that of the Palace, is "invisible," an order "not in the least concerned with appearances."

Jeremy Bentham's Panopticon, initially conceived in 1787 and finally rejected by Parliament twenty years later, was, in the mind of its philosopher-inventor, the foundation for a stable social system. Even the name of the project—the all-seeing eye—grew out of Bentham's preoccupation with controlling human behavior to improve the human condition, by design.[22]

The Panopticon and the Palace each constitute an apparatus of covert control based on the manipulation of lines of sight.

Bentham's design limited these lines via solid masonry construction and centralized organization. In his original scheme of 1787 prisoners located in a peripheral ring of cells were illuminated in such a way as to be seen by a governor located at the center of the plan. This light shone down at a precise angle between prisoner and governor preventing the former any view of their overseers. The governor's invisibility was enhanced in the second scheme of 1791,

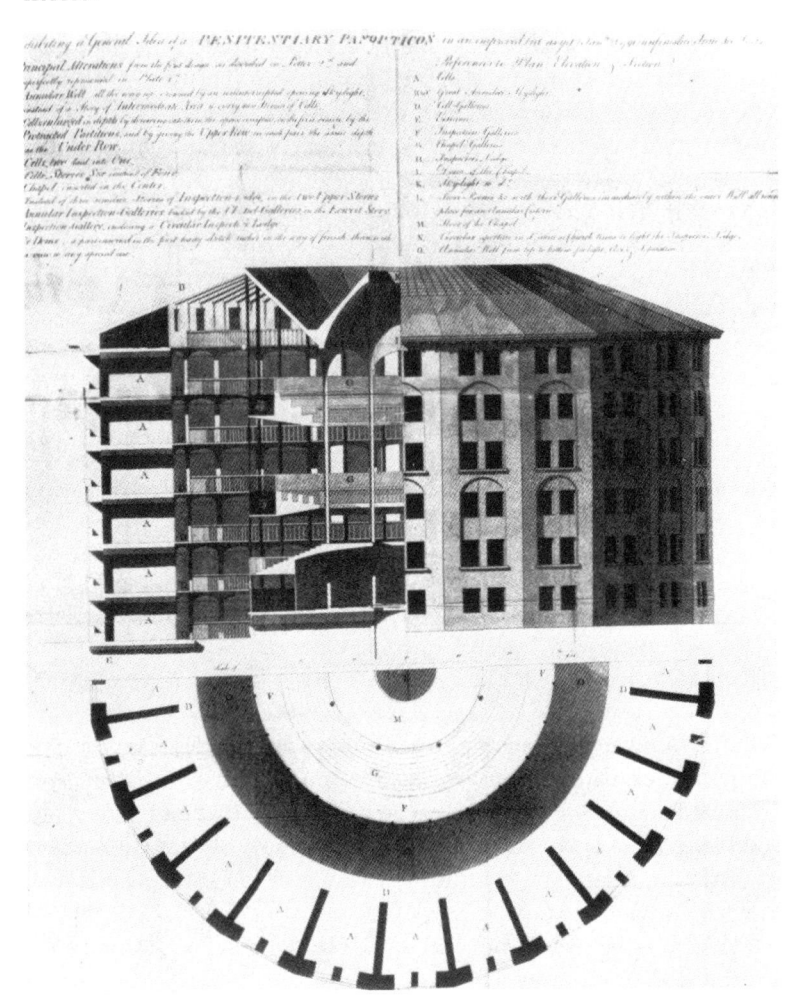

9. *Penetentiary Panopticon*, section, elevation, and half-plan.

where circular hallways for turnkeys were located between the cells and the central core. This design allowed the inspectors to be invisible from the prisoners; from a centralized position the governor could watch the movement of both.

In the Panopticon, position was central to the surveillance mechanism.[23] The invisible order of Bentham's design is predicated on the same principles as perspectival representation. Both depend upon the inscription of a set of fixed relationships between points—relationships of power. The prison utilized the cone of vision to constrain and facilitate observation; the unique station point (in perspective also known as the "viewing point") was the governor's privileged location. Like the man in Vignola's *Regola di Perspectiva*, the governor was the source of sight lines mapping exclusive power over the objects of his gaze. The anisotropic nature of the Panopticon's surveillance apparatus clearly sited the locus of control.

The Panopticon exerted its power openly. With solid masonry on the exterior, it signaled an exclusive, private place in an otherwise public realm. The penitentiary did use iron and glass, although only in the interior atrium, where they supported explicit sociopolitical and moral agendas. To cite Evans:

> The combination of iron, or steel and glass to create unified, brightly illuminated interior spaces is familiar in modern architecture. What is less familiar is the early appearance of the same combination as part of a scheme to impose an unremitting rule on the patterns of human action. The function of inspection was greatly enhanced by the use of these materials. With masonry nothing like the same panorama could have been achieved. Considerations of economy and aesthetics played their part, but his eminently modern construction was justified primarily in terms of a philosophy of government, based on an idea about the way the human mind worked. In other words it was an essay in the engineering of behavior through the manipulation of architectural form.[24]

The ferro-vitreous atrium enclosed the interior space of inspection and engineered reformation.

The Crystal Palace engineered power differently: the distinction between the observer and the observed was not clear. Instead of circumscribing a single locus of control, analogous to the recognizable authority of a single ruler or elected political body, it removed all visible and spatial references to the existence of a governing force. Paxton's design multiplied rather than restricted possible lines of site. Its power derived from diffusion rather than constraint. The linear organization of the hall did not suggest hierarchically framed views or any one privileged place. The variable surface activity of the glass skin continually deflected or distracted attention and hence "weakened" all eyes equally.

The Crystal Palace dispensed with the fixed relationships essential to the Panopticon. With an infinite number of vanishing points, the Crystal Palace finds its analogue in the object-oriented axonometric rather than the subjectively based perspectival construction. In Paxton's project and in three- dimensional orthographic projections exact positioning relative to an external point is rendered immaterial. As Ciucci has noted, "If perspective was the instrument to manage and organize human space, descriptive geometry is the instrument to manage and organize industrial space."[25] While descriptive geometry was never wholly embraced by architects (most likely because of its extreme abstraction), its more concrete cousin, axonometric projection, was the preferred mode of representation of modern space. The axonometric represents the object as seen from an infinite distance implying an omniscient viewer. Like painted panoramas or hot-air balloon photographs whose images frame an area too broad to be seen by the unaided human eye, the axonometric is divorced from the restrictions imposed by human perception.

What the "limited power of human art" (more specifically, the art of perspective) precluded in Bentham's Panopticon was in fact achieved in the Crystal Palace. The design of the Crystal Palace was predicated on a limitless field of vision, rather than one structured by a line, or a cone. It implied an unrestrained scope of power, as free from spatial constraints as current global advertising campaigns that operate from afar and ignore specific sociocultural circumstances in their search for ever larger markets. This unlimited power was concealed by the ideals associated with transparency and by its physical nature, which combined to project a vision of the building as morally correct as well as socially and spatially inclusive. On the surface, the Crystal Palace seemed to overcome the fundamentally enclosive, and thereby exclusive, condition of architecture. Yet, its literal and phenomenal transparency created a distraction (doubly masked by the apparent lack of architectural distraction) according the building exactly that covert power discussed by Benjamin.

From the exterior, the Palace appeared equally accessible to all, presenting everyone the same opportunity to see and be seen; inside, it embroiled consumer and commodity alike in the game of consumption. Like the "natural" landscapes of the picturesque, the clear glass Palace posed as something it was not. The opportunity to see and be seen provided the masses with a false sense of power that obscured their economic powerlessness; it provided them with visual treats (carefully protected in their own glass boxes) to fuel desires that could never be satisfied. The seemingly innocent and pure crystal building was an insidious player in a game of capitalist power and control.

THE INVISIBLE MASK

You even begin vaguely to fear something.—Fyodor Dostoevski

In Dostoevski's *Notes from Underground* we read, "You believe in the crystal edifice indestructible for all eternity, the kind that you could never stick your tongue out at on the sly or thumb your nose at secretly. Well, perhaps the reason I am afraid of that edifice is that it is crystal and indestructible for all eternity and one can't even stick one's tongue out at it on the sly."[26] The ideals of modernity embodied by the Crystal

Palace that so enthused Giedion, Hitchcock, and countless others are construed very differently by Dostoevski. If architects praised the Palace for the secrets it brought to light, to Dostoevski it was damned for exactly the same reason. The "Underground Man," despite his parodic intentions, uncovers what the crystalline structure masks: the transparent material's fragility hides an indestructibility rooted in the fact that it offers no place to sneer unnoticed.

A glass building denies the safety of the interior by emptying it; it offers no protection, no place of escape, no space for private reflection.[27] As Richard Sennett has written, such architecture is hostile to the individual: "Far from being neutral, the space created by the architecture of glass is highly charged. It is space that in its hostility to livability, in its very hostility to nature, seeks to consecrate itself—to become sacred, inviolable . . . an architecture which in its very inhospitableness, creates a privileged position for itself. This is the highest, most arrogant privilege."[28]

Glass architecture erects a divisive barrier between the senses. As Dostoevski observed, its power is manifest in its capacity to silence. Standing on one side of any glazed wall—a cafe, shop window, or glass office tower—one suffers a peculiar form of sensory deprivation. A glass wall lets one see but not touch, see but not hear, see but not speak. (The final frames of "The Graduate"—with Dustin Hoffman trapped, screaming behind a transparent wall at the wrong end of the wedding chapel—powerfully illustrate the divisive nature of glass.) In the case of the Crystal Palace, this divisiveness was enhanced by the structure's monumentality. Monumentality can be understood as the erasure of scale that leaves viewer and building without common measure. The enormous Crystal edifice acquired authority by virtue of its unapproachableness. Clues to its scale could be discovered in the Palace's modular iron structure: to see a frame is to recognize that which is framed—the glass. When the contents of the frame are transparent—invisible—one looks past or through the absent picture plane. When the number of frames is infinite, no prospect is distinguished over another and the power of the frame to guide the eye is diminished. As the iron framework yields to the park beyond, its function as a scaling device is quite literally, overlooked. The glass itself, of course, offers no means of establishing scale. Bucher writes:

> We see a delicate network of lines without any clue by means of which we might judge their distance from the eye or the real size; we cannot tell if this structure towers a hundred feet or a thousand feet above us or whether the roof is a flat platform or is built up from a succession of ridges, for there is no play of shadows to enable our optic nerves to gauge the measurements.[29]

In spite of its transparency—through and because of it—the building is not "sightable." This inexplicable quality is the result of a doubling operation: the viewer—empowered on one hand to control the building, to see through the structure, to cut through its skin and view the interior—is stripped of power by the same transparency that makes it impossible to "stick one's tongue out at it on the sly." Using the ambiguity of transparency, the Palace set up a confrontation between two lines of sight: the trajectory into and through the skin is poised against lines of sight emitted out from the same transparent surface. In the isotropic Palace, the ideal of transparency folds back onto itself; the viewer cannot escape the condition of being viewed.

The idealized, pure, and morally correct transparency so important to Rousseau and the Glass Chain architects is shattered by Dostoevski's realization that the palace, far from benign, exerts a covert power. It precludes questioning, and in turn requires total submission. Foreclosing the right to react, the building assumes a political force. Like the wearer of the Ring of Gyges, the Crystal Palace is itself all-seeing. Herein lies its "arrogant privilege."

Gerhard Auer has recently written "Before the other senses assert their rights, it is the eye that takes possession of things."[30] Possessing the world through vision renders the chaotic comprehensible and from this sense of understanding comes a sense of control. Taken together, Dostoevski's reaction and Buchers description point to an inversion. In the Crystal Palace, the eye cannot take possession of the building. The building takes possession of the eye. This presents a paradox: according to Benjamin, architecture does not absorb its viewers but is absorbed by them. By controlling the eye, on the other hand, architecture determines not only what we see, but how. It shapes a conception of the world and ways of living in that world.

All architecture—transparent or not—configures form and material in spatial constructs with ideological force. All architecture—whether it houses explicitly political programs or not—politicizes space. A uniform grid that flattens differences and a chaotic "strip" marked by extreme difference and the complete lack of an organizing structure are not purely formal orders. They are physical constructs with political analogues.

Architecture allied to institutions of power, like Bentham's Panopticon, is expected to function as an apparatus of control. The acknowledgement of its capacity to reinforce a ruling authority provides the necessary awareness to confront, criticize, and even counteract its power. Despite an equal capacity to regulate and control, architecture with apparently non political programs such as Paxton's Crystal Palace is rarely viewed politically. Overlooking

THE INVISIBLE MASK

architecture's tacit politic, architects and viewers alike are subject to a covert power; the former by failing to confront the essentially ideological nature of their work and therefore abdicating their political responsibility and the latter by dismissing the regulatory effects of architecture.

The tacit politic of architecture and its capacity to wield covert power raise a number of questions: What constitutes the invisible apparatus of control? What exactly is received incidentally? Why are these politics overlooked and by whom? What is the role of the architect and what are the effects of architectural work?

There is still a profound resistance on the part of architects to the notion that their forms are in fact ideologically and politically loaded; that physical constructs enclose, foreclose, or disclose abstract relations of power. Acknowledging these conditions will not necessarily lead to answers to the above questions; nor will it ensure that architecture becomes politically correct (whatever that might mean). But it will allow architects to proceed ethically, informed by the consciousness that they deploy power and able to question openly the ends to which that power is put.

1. Walter Benjamin, "Art in the Age of Mechanical Reproduction," *Illuminations* (New York: Schocken Books, 1989), 240.
2. Sigfried Giedion, *Space, Time and Architecture: The Growth of a New Tradition* (Cambridge: Harvard University Press, 1969), 251.
3. Giedion, *Space, Time and Architecture*, 306.
4. From the April 1850 W. Bridges Adams's *Westminster and Foreign Quarterly Review* cited in John Hix, *The Glass House* (Cambridge: MIT Press, 1974), 133.
5. The Crystal Palace exhibits four of the seven characteristics of the arcade noted by J. F. Geist: a skylit space, a system of access, a form of organizing retail trade, and a space of transition. Johann Friedrich Giest, *Arcades, The History of a Building Type*, (Cambridge: MIT Press, 1983), 12.
6. For a discussion of Haussmann's boulevards as they created a space of public spectacle see T. J. Clark, *The Painting of Modern Life* (New York. Knopf, 1985).
7. Steven Daniels, "The Political Iconography of Woodland" in Cosgrove and Daniels, *The Iconography of Landscape* (Cambridge: Cambridge University Press, 1988), 73. It is interesting to note here an arcane usage of "policy" (a term etymologically tied to politics) taken from the Oxford English Dictionary: "The improvement and embellishment of an estate, building, town, etc.; property created by human skill or labor."
8. Walter Benjamin, "Paris, Capital of the Nineteenth Century," *Reflections* (New York: Harcourt Brace Jovanovich, 1978), 153.
9. Marshall Berman, *All That is Solid Melts into Air: The Experience of Modernity* (New York: Simon & Schuster, 1982), 237.
10. Georg Kohlmaier and Barbara von Sartory, *Houses of Glass: A Nineteenth Century Building Type* (Cambridge: MIT Press, 1981), 305.
11. Lothar Bucher, cited in Giedion, *Space, Time and Architecture*, 253.

12. Nikolaus Pevsner, *Pioneers of Modern Design* (New York: Penguin, 1979), 135.
13. Henry-Russell Hitchcock Jr., "The British Nineteenth Century and Modern Architecture," *Modern Architecture in England* (New York: The Museum of Modern Art, 1937), 10.
14. Colin Rowe and Robert Slutzky, "Transparency: Literal and Phenomenal" reprinted in *Mathematics of the Ideal Villa* (Cambridge: MIT Press, 1976).
15. Anthony Vidler, *The Writing of The Walls* (Princeton: Princeton Architectural Press, 1987), 112.
16. Paul Scheerbart, *Glass Architecture*, excerpted in Ulrich Conrad, *Programs and Manifestoes on 20th-century Architecture* (Cambridge: MIT Press, 1964), 32.
17. Francesco Dal Co and Manfredo Tafuri, *Modern Architecture* (New York: Abrams, 1976), 129.
18. Ralph Lieberman, "The Crystal Palace," *AAFiles* 12 (London: Architectural Association, 1976), 55.
19. Giedion, *Space, Time and Architecture*, 252.
20. Jean Starobinski, *Jean Jacques Rousseau* (Chicago: University of Chicago Press, 1988), 255.
21. Starobinski, *Jean Jacques Rousseau*, 255.
22. For the following description of Jeremy Bentham's Panopticon, I am indebted to Robin Evan's discussion of the project in *The Fabrication of Virtue: English Prison Architecture 1750-1840* (Cambridge: Cambridge University, 1982).
23. On the inspection principles in prison design: "The panopticon brought surveillance to a new perfection. Yet by introducing more and more inspection, more and more pervasive control, by orienting every aspect of design and construction to this one advantage and condensing the prison into a single volume he changed the nature of the principle itself . . . in the panopticon [surveillance] became the very source of morality." Evans, *The Fabrication of Virtue*, 211.
24. Evans, *The Fabrication of Virtue*, 222.
25. Giorgo Ciucci, "The Representation of Space and the Space of Representation," in *Rappresentazioni, Rassegna* 9, Anno IV (March 1982): 7-18.
26. Fyodor Doestoevski, *Notes From Underground* (Boston: University Press of America, 1969), 34.
27. For a discussion of the effects of glass on the architectural interior see Jose Quetglas, "Fear of Glass: The Barcelona Pavilion," in *Architectureproduction* (New York: Princeton Architectural Press, 1988), 122-152.
28. Richard Sennet, "The Glass Age," reprinted in *Harpers Magazine* (June 1989): 14-19.
29. Lothar Bucher cited by Marshall Berman, *All That is Solid Melts into Air* (New York: Simon and Schuster, 1982) 239.
30. Gerhard Auer, "Editorial," *Daidalos* 33 (Sept., 1989): 25.

ANN BERGREN

BAUBO AND HELEN:
GENDER IN THE IRREPARABLE WOUND

"Is it true that dear God is present everywhere?" a little girl asked her mother, "but I find that indecent"—a hint for philosophers! One should hold in greater honor the shame (Scham) with which nature has hidden herself behind riddles and iridescent uncertainties. Is truth perhaps a woman who has reasons not to let her reasons be seen? Is her name perhaps—to speak Greek—Baubo? —Nietzsche[1]

INTRODUCTION

I would like to examine two elements of the problem Stanley Tigerman has set for our conference: the notion of an "irreparable wound" and that of "re-writing/righting" it.

What wounds cannot be repaired? Death and castration. And one other. The blood-letting gash taken to be the *eidolon* "image, ghost" of castration. To gaze as a man upon the irreparable wound

---

This text was originally written for the 1988 Chicago Forum on Architectural Issues, sponsored by the Association of Collegiate Schools of Architecture, "Looking for America, Part III: Failed Attempts to Heal an Irreparable Wound." The conference was designed by Stanley Tigerman to "examine the intersection between critical theory and architecture in regard to humankind's instinctive optimism that leads us to attempt healing in various, it is hoped, architectural ways." The proceedings will comprise the third portion of the forthcoming book, *Looking for America*, to be published by Rizzoli. This essay is reprinted here with their permission.

of death and castration is to see the intersection (where Oedipus killed his father)—the intersection of death and castration with the (w)hole of life.

Tigerman's graphic pun "re-write/right" contains two responses— two different "genders" of response—to the "irreparable wound."

One is "to re-right."[2] To make right, to make whole and like new again, obliterating all trace of suture, leaving no scar. To put the castrated phallus back up right—and thereby to re-build an opposition between the absence and the presence of: phallus, (w)holeness, substance, materiality.

The other response is "to re-write." To draw, to cut, to construct the irreparable wound again, repeating the wound, mirroring the wound with its image. To match the bleeding genital with its *eidolon*: (w)holeness. A trope, a *tropos* "turning" of the wound into its figure.

Each response—re-righting and re-writing (it is a graphic—and architectural—fact that I cannot indicate which response I mean by speaking these words alone: to avoid the collapse of the difference between the two, I have to construct a spoken difference, a differentiating pun: re-(up)righting for re-righting)—each of thes responses risks repeating the structure of the wound.

Re-(up)righting risks setting up right again Platonic metaphysics and its psychoanalytic counterpart. It risks re-arming the weapon that inflicts the wound.

A re-writing of the wound risks repeating itself. It risks provoking laughter or violence, a rape by the weapon just re-armed. For, architecturally, there can be no re-writing without a re-(up)righting.

Both responses find their analogue in the ancient Greek figure of Baubo, an image of the "irreparable wound." When women see her, they re-write her. When men see her, they run to re-(up)righting.

BAUBO

In Greek myth Demeter is the goddess of marriage, childbirth, and the fertility of the earth. When her daughter Persephone is raped by Hades, the goddess reacts by abnegating her powers. She disguises herself as a mortal—an old woman, past child-bearing age, who is in mourning. She wanders the earth until she arrives at Eleusis, where her Mysteries will be established. There she is received by the queen named Baubo who offers the stranger *xenia* "hospitality" in an exchange that would make the stranger— the "other"—a member of one's "own."[3] But the mourning goddess refuses to eat or drink.[4] At this refusal, Baubo lifts her skirts and exposes her genitals. At this sight, the goddess Demeter laughs. She then eats and drinks, and the fertility of women and of the earth returns.

Although she has no explicit iconography in ancient art, various images have been identified with Baubo by virtue of representing her characteristic gesture—the exposure of the genitals on a figure either nude or raising her skirt in the *anasurma* ("lifting up"), as it is termed by historians of ancient art and myth. These include terra-cotta figurines that appear to have been used in the exclusively female rituals of Demeter (figs. 1 and 2),[5] where they enabled a woman to see her *sexe* not directly (as a man can see his), but in "mirrors" such as these.

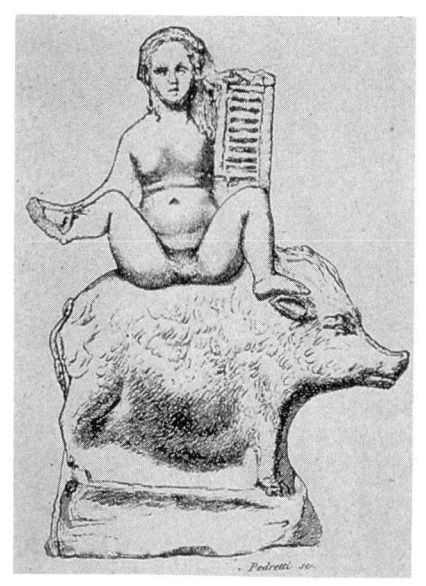

1. South Italian terracotta figurine, identified with Baubo. With her knees bent in the position of childbirth, the female rides a pig, an animal sacred to Demeter.
2. Terracotta figurine with torch, identified with Baubo, found in the precinct of Demeter at Priene. 4th-century B.C.

In both myth and ritual, the reaction of the female spectator to Baubo is itself a mirroring—a re-writing. At the unveiling of the woman's (w)hole, women open their mouths. They open themselves to the exchanges of *xenia*, to taking in and to giving out. Above, they laugh. They eat and drink. Below, they play Baubo themselves, exposing their (w)holes to impregnation and to giving birth.

What happens when the viewer of Baubo is male? When it is the object of the "male gaze," the exposure of the female genitals functions in antiquity and in later European culture as the apotropaic gesture *par excellence*.[6] In men the *anasurma* produces fear and

109

flight. For, as Freud observes in his notes on the "Medusa's Head" (*SE* X.105-106), "what arouses horror in oneself will produce the same effect upon the enemy against whom one is seeking to defend oneself. We read in Rabelais of how the Devil took to flight when the woman showed him her vulva."—an occasion memorably captured in an illustration from the Fables of La Fontaine (fig. 3).[7]

3. Illustration from La Fontaine's *Fables*. Charles Eisen, illustrator (ca. 1750)

After he flees in fright from Baubo, what does the male do then? How is such flight related to "re-(up)righting?" They are related by the twin metonymies of repression and displacement. In instances from Greek mythopoeic and philosophical thought, the male runs from the sight/site of Baubo to re-erect the phallus in another place. In the context of gender as constructed according to Platonic philosophics and Freudian psychoanalytics, the apotropaic force of the *anasyrma* is a reflection of castration anxiety. This anxiety seeks relief in a certain architecture—a new placement, a re-(up)righting that will repress the wound without a trace. Such re-(up)righting builds a difference, a (gender) difference between the wound and the erection, between absence and presence. It becomes the non-original origin of (gender) difference as an architecture of re-pres(s)ence. Built as it is upon a repression, however, such re-construction is liable to earthquake.

What threatens to return from under any re-(up)righting is re-writing—the face of Baubo, the irreparable wound itself, the non-original origin of difference as a quasi-architectural absence.

The face of the wound returns as its double in the structure of what is used to heal wounds—the drug or *pharmakon*—the structure of the *tropos* "turning." Baubo returns as the construction of inevitable re-turn. Greek thought reveals and controls the uncontrollability of this pharmacological structure in the figure of another female, Helen.

HELEN AND HOMERIC EPIC:
THE TROPOLOGY OF THE *PHARMAKON*

In the *Odyssey*, when Telemachus visits Sparta to learn about his father Odysseus, Helen and Menelaus respond with the *xenia* "hospitality" of a banquet.[8] At the dinner Menelaus's stories of the Greeks' suffering at Troy and of the apparent loss of Odysseus provoke lamentation that threatens to turn the feast into a funeral. So Helen attempts to turn the evening from stories of Iliadic tragedy into Odyssean laughter. She spikes the wine with a "good drug" from Egypt that can keep a man from weeping even at the sight of his mother or father or brother or son being slaughtered before his eyes.[9] She then adds a story of her own in praise of Odysseus.

4. Marilyn Monroe—a "daughter of Helen"—giving birth to the world under the roof of her legs.

Like her "good drug," Helen's story attempts a rhetoric of replacement—a re-pres(s)entation of the past without pain. She tells how Odysseus came into Troy on a spy mission, disguised as a beggar, how she alone recognized him, and how she rejoiced at the deaths of those he killed leaving the city, while the other Trojan women mourned, since her heart had returned to the side of the Greeks and the handsome husband she had left behind. Thus Helen flatters both her husband and her guest, the son of that successful spy—and herself, just as she once seduced Paris, another young guest, and can ever re-seduce her husband by producing reality as he wants to hear it (fig. 4).

But Helen does not remain sitting on top of the world. Working under the power of the *pharmakon*, Helen's story engenders a doublet, as Menelaus begins to praise Odysseus himself. In his story Menelaus recalls how of all the Greeks hidden in the Trojan Horse, only Odysseus was able to resist calling out, when Helen, with Deiphobus by her side, imitated the voices of their wives. And who was this Deiphobus? He was Helen's second Trojan husband, the man she married *after* the death of Paris, a figure who belies her claim that when Odysseus infiltrated the city, her allegiance had returned to the Greeks. By permitting Menelaus to recall without pain what pain might have kept beyond recall, Helen's "good drug" recoils upon its practitioner. In attempting to divide drugs and poetry into governable opposites, and to apply an antidote of pleasure and glory to the pain and death of the war fought to re-possess her, Helen's cure succeeds and by that success wounds again.

HELEN AND STESICHORUS
EIDOLON AND *ETUMOS LOGOS*, BLINDNESS (CASTRATION) AND INSIGHT

The tropology of the *pharmakon* belongs as well to Helen herself. She embodies an ethical and ontological ambivalence that the poet Stesichorus attempted to master. In the *Phaedrus* (243a) Plato reports with approval how Stesichorus, like Homer, was blinded, after his slander of Helen. But unlike Homer, Stesichorus recovered his sight by composing a *palinoidia* "recantation': "this account (*logos*) is not true (*etumos*), you did not embark upon the well-oared ships, you did not come to the citadel of Troy." If the true Helen never went to Troy, for whom did the armies fight and die? In the *Republic* (586c) Plato says that "phantoms of true pleasure" (*eidola tes alethous hedones*) cause themselves to be fought over "just as Stesichorus says that the *eidolon* ('image, ghost') of Helen was fought over by those at Troy in ignorance of the truth (*alethous*)." It was the *eidolon* of Helen that went to Troy; the true Helen was in Egypt.

This abbreviated anecdote is like a mystery: what does it mean? But like a dream, it speaks in decipherable clues. To say that Helen left her husband and went with Paris to Troy is to lift her skirts, to show what really happened there. It is to open the house of Menelaus and expose what is really inside—not the phallus firmly planted (like the living tree of Odysseus's marriage bed) in a stable female foundation, but a place where the ground has slipped out from underneath (a woman exchanged in marriage who does not stay put), leaving phallus and *oikos* disconnected and in collapse. It is to reveal the sight/site of castration. As such, the revelation results in blindness, castration's displaced analogue. Like Helen's "good drug" as a remedy of tragedy, Stesichorus's antidote—his construction of the opposition between the *eidolon* and the *etumos logos*—cures the castration/blindness. But by curing, it returns as truth what was repressed as false, turning itself into fantasy.

For just as Helen's story evokes Menelaus's contradiction, Stesichorus's construction evokes the parallel, but confuting, case of Tiresias. Tiresias received the gift of prophecy from Zeus and blindness from Zeus's wife Hera, for having seen and spoken the secret truth—the *etumos logos*—of female sexuality, namely that it is greater than the male's.[10] His blindness re-writes the truth of his sight of the female genital. The figure of Tiresias thus turns Stesichorus into another Oedipus, whose sight depends upon repressing his sight of the female genital (that of his mother and wife) and who will blind himself when he is forced to see again. Despite his admiration for Stesichorus's palinodic strategy, Plato will attempt to save himself from its fate—the collapse of opposition into inebriated tropology in which blindness is insight, and the non-material figure—the *eidolon*—reveals the truth.

THE *EIDOLON* IN PLATONIC PHILOSOPHY
PLATONIC ARCHITECTURAL THEORY: RE-(UP)RIGHTING VS. RE-WRITING
Platonic philosophy attempts a re-(up)righting of Stesichorus's collapsed palinode by constructing the figure of a philosopher-architect, one who constructs a stable division between *etumos logos* and the *eidolon* by dividing the *eidolon* into two categories. This apparently original "design solution" in fact repeats the structure of the *pharmakon*.

In *The Sophist*, Plato sets up two kinds of the *eidolopoiike techne* "*eidolon*-making or image-making art"—two kinds of *mimesis* "imitation." First is the single, accurate copy of the Form—it is *heteron* "other than," but *eikos* "like" to its *paradigma* "paradigm," and so is the *eikon* "likeness, icon" of its Formal model. Second is that which "appears" (*phainetai*) to be like its paradigm, but is not, and so is only an *phantasma* "appearance" (*Sophist* 235b-236b). There can be only one true *eikon* "likeness, icon'—as there is only one Odysseus, one true husband of Penelope. But as there are many Suitors, there are myriad phantasms, illegitimate pretenders to the status of true copy.[11]

The maker of the *phantasma* "appearance"-kind of *eidolon* "image" is the sophist. The sophist is like a Suitor. He imitates, knowing he has only an opinion and no true knowledge of the Form (*Sophist* 264c-268d). The philosopher-architect, in contrast, is like Odysseus. As divine *demiourgos* "artisan" of the cosmos in the *Timaeus*, he builds only the *eikon* "likeness, icon"-kind of *eidolon* "image," the true imitation of a Form. The Demiurge "constructs"[12] the world as the one true, sensible copy of the one true world of intelligible Forms. In the same way, his human counterpart, whether building a house or drawing its *eidolon*—that "other house, a man-made dream for those awake" (*Sophist* 266c-d)—imitates the Form he knows.

The Platonic philosopher-architect would thus transcend the dichotomy between Tiresias and Oedipus—between the truth as non-material *eidolon*, seen only with the mind's eye, the truth as castration, seen only in blindness, and the truth as seen in every material presence except the material absence in the face of Baubo. Like Perseus looking away from Medusa, the Platonic philosopher-architect would build with the insight of Tiresias only what Oedipus sees (not the sight he represses and is blinded with when forced to see). By building a true material *eidolon* of the nonmaterial Form, the Platonic philosopher-architect could displace all material images lacking the support of Formal truth. He could substitute a pure *eikon* for a *phantasma*. He could heal the wound without a trace. He could re-(up)right without re-writing.

This philosophical construction is an architectural theory—an allegorical program for architectural practice. Platonic architectural theory would not limit practice to the imitation of geometrical Forms. Rather, as human analogue to the divine demiurge, the Platonic architect-philosopher would be able to imitate, whether in three-dimensional building or in two-dimensional drawing, any Form that he as philosopher-architect knows, any Form that he knows will conform to the architectural laws of an architectural Form, any Form he can draw or build. He would not have to re-write castration. He could heal the irreparable wound by building what he knows will stand up right.

KATE MANTILINI RESTAURANT, MORPHOSIS

The Kate Mantilini Restaurant designed by Morphosis offers an opportunity to track this Platonic "attempt to heal an irreparable wound." To question the healing art of a building is to invoke its relation to client, context, and use, as well as its architectural rhetoric—both conscious and unconscious.

BAUBO AND HELEN

The client of "Kate's" is Marilyn Lewis, co-founder and CEO of the highly commercial, highly successful restaurant chain of Hamburger Hamlets. Marilyn Lewis wanted to build a restaurant named for a woman about whom she had heard stories as a girl. Kate Mantilini was the Irish-Italian mistress of Lewis's uncle and a boxing promoter during the forties and fifties in Cleveland, a woman who profited independently from the love and the aggression of men. Lewis wanted the building to recall the time "when people dressed up to go to the fights and went to a great chophouse afterwards." She envisioned a place evocative of White's Diners and Edward Hopper paintings. In the building she paid for (figs. 5-6), did she get what she wanted or needed?

5. Kate Mantilini Restaurant. Exterior   6. Interior.

The Kate Mantilini Restaurant devotes itself to supplanting commercialism and nostalgic populism with architectural grandeur. It is a *Gesamtkunstwerk* "total art work" including painting and sculpture—a self-reflexive cosmos (like that of *Timaeus*) relentlessly dramatizing its own architectural process, a built reminder that glamour and grammar come from the same root.

The building's meta-architectural achievement is most clear in the sculptural collage of its structural, formal, material, and graphic elements suspended below a glass-enclosed vault (fig. 7). Three strips of grey steel, backed by a sheet of corrugated metal, travel on a line with the three grey boxing-ring ropes in John Wehrle's time-lapse mural of the final moment of the 1985 Hagler-Hearns championship fight in Los Vegas. The steel strips curve around where fragments of the mural are repeated in reverse temporal order. In both mural and fragment, the fighters are followed by a ballerina in arabesque— the building's sole female reference, apart from its sign.

In front of this metamorphosis from mural to metal to mural again is a configuration of steel pieces that reflects the "building within a building" composition of Kate's (fig.8). The restaurant is a renovation of a fifties bank, with a new interior structure analyzing the formal potentialities of the old rectangular shell. Rising from the booths, a thick *poché* wall parallels the thin line of original columns, while the booths at the far corner and the monumental doorway rotate off the old building's axis, and the back wall countermands the straightness opposite with the mural's protruding curve. Correspondingly, in the sculpture, a cut-out, rectangular plane of brownish steel traces the plan of the building's original shell. Both beside and askew of the two-dimensional rectangle hangs a gray, three-dimensional frame. The sides of this piece are cut-out trapezoids, four-sided forms let loose from rectilinear axiality. Jutting out from the brown rectangular plane—as if sucked in from the building's exterior trabeation—is a single beam. The whole sculpture is a conceptual magnet, pulling to itself and holding in analytical suspension elements from all over the building.

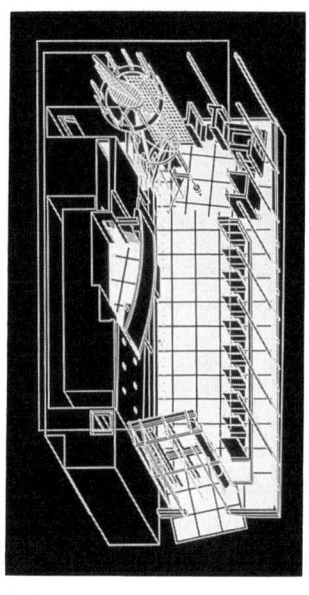

7. Sculpture   8. Axonometric Drawing

But the sculpture is also a source, a material *mimesis* of the architect's mind at work, with the elements of his language—the Forms he knows—held in pre-syntactical readiness, temporally and spatially displaced and condensed, as in the Lacanian subconscious. This model of the architectural mind is not static, but moves toward its primary articulation in the graphic, as the sculpture reaches the ground as stylus, wheel, and drawing (figs. 9 and 10). The configuration implies a certain temporality: that the wheel, now at rest, was moved by the energy of the designing mind, embodied in the conceptual fragments above, to draw the plan on the floor.

The Kate Mantilini Restaurant is not a postmodern fragment of Marilyn Lewis's past. It serves rather to suppress her memories (the specifics of Kate Mantilini's life and the style of forties and fifties diners) under an *eidolon*—an image and imitation—of its own formal origins. So why, then, did she pay for it? How does it satisfy her desires? By its stunning success in suppressing the iconography of commercialism, Kate's has become a huge commercial success. People are drawn to eat there by its architectural glamour. By building pure meta-architecture, Kate's has reinscribed itself within the materialistic enterprise it eschews. By its re-(up)righting, it re-writes what it erases.

9. Sculpture terminating in wheel, stylus, and drawing
10. Detail of Wheel, stylus and drawing

The Kate Mantilini Restaurant reveals the pharmacological structure imperfectly repressed within the Platonic architectural program. Like Helen's "good drug" and Stesichorus's palinode, Kate's restaurant succeeds in a repression that returns the repressed. With all the irony of high and low in Los Angeles, the building has turned into an *eidolon* of a twenty-first-century cult center, a place of ritual and myth, a space for repeated eating and drinking under the aegis of an eponymous heroine, whose story is told and retold to newcomers by enthusiastic waiters. Is it symptomatic of Kate's success that the architects regard its sign as a failure?

FORM BECOMES EVENT IN STOIC PHILOSOPHY
TROPING PLATONIC ARCHITECTURAL THEORY:
RE-(UP)RIGHTING AS RE-WRITING

As post-Greek philosophy has aimed to this day at a *reversement* of Plato, so we may conceive of a *reversement* of Platonic architectural theory: not re-(up)righting without re-writing, but re-(up)righting as re-writing; not fear and flight from the sight and site of Baubo—repressing one pole of the *pharmakon* only to return the other—not fear and flight, division and repression, but the risk of re-constructing the "irreparable wound" itself.

Such is the architectural program in the Stoic reversal of Platonic metaphysics as analyzed by Gilles Deleuze.[13] Stoic ontology distinguishes two categories. The first consists of bodies and states of bodies. They take the linguistic form of nouns and adjectives. Each body is a cause of the other, the sum of their mutual causality being Fate. These corporeal things exist. The second category consists of the effects of these bodies as causes. They take the linguistic form of verbs. The effects are incorporeal events, the sum of their connection being Necessity. They do not exist, but—in Deleuze's term—they "insist."[14]

The two categories differ in their temporality. The first category, that of bodes and states of bodies, is a living present, encompassing past and future, the time of a gerund—like "building," for example. The time of the second, that of incorporeal events, is an infinitive—like "to build," for example.[15] The time of the incorporeal event is a "to become, to happen" (*devenir*) that eludes the center and thus does not separate past and future. It is an in-finitive, in-finitely divided, going simultaneously in the two "senses" (both "meanings" and "directions") of past and future at once.[16]

The French *sens* "sense, meaning" allows Deleuze to capture both the spatiotemporal and the epistemological force of the infinitival event: it goes in both *sens*, in both senses or directions at once—in contrast to the *bon sens* "good sense, meaning" of a *sens unique* "one-way street, univocal meaning" or a *sens commun* "common sense."[17] For example, in a body, the infinitival event is the "to be cut"—the "wound" itself.[18] The event is not being, but a manner of being, on the surface of the corporeal body.[19]

This Stoic ontology accomplishes a reversal of Plato. Now material things—bodies—constitute being and substance. So the characteristics of the incorporeal Platonic Form fall upon the side of the event.[20] In the Stoic event—the incorporeal effect upon the surface of the body—we find a return of the repressed Platonic *phantasma*—the return of Helen and/as *eidolon*[21]—now with the status previously held by the Platonic Form, that of nonmaterial truth.

The event is the mode of the *tropos* and the *pharmakon*, the mode of infinite reversal. As an effect only, it is absolutely impassive. In it, therefore, active and passive—for example, "to cut" and "to be cut"—are exchanged. In its infinite escape of the present, the event is both past and future—"cut too deeply" and "not cut enough"—and both effect and quasi-cause—"scar" and "wound." Deleuze explains:

Unlimited becoming [*le devenir-illimit*] becomes the event itself, ideal and incorporeal, with all of its characteristic reversals between future and past, active and passive, cause and effect, more and less, too much and not enough, already and not yet. The infinitely divisible event is always *both at once*. It is eternally that which has just happened and that which is about to happen, but never that which is happening (to cut too deeply and not enough). The event, being itself impassive, allows the active and the passive to be interchanged more easily, since it is *neither the one nor the other*, but rather their common result (to cut—to be cut). Concerning the cause and the effect, events, *being always only effects*, are better able to form among themselves functions of quasi-causes or relations of quasi-causality which are always reversible (the wound and the scar).[22]

This view of the "irreparable wound" implies a certain ethics.

The aim of Stoic morality is to extricate from every state of corporeal things the pure event, and to will it. This mode of volition should not be confused with resignation, which is merely another form of impotent, immoral *ressentiment*.[23] Rather, Stoic liberty is a sort of troping. The will directed by Stoic wisdom "attains the point where war is waged against war, the wound is traced living as the scar of all wounds, and death is returned willed against all deaths."[24] The human being is an actor whose role is "counter-effectuation" (*contre-effectuation*) of the event as effect.[25] It is the comic role of attaching to "plagues, tyrannies, and the most ghastly wars the comic chance of having reigned for nothing."[26] The comedy produced is revolutionary freedom, both individual and social.[27]

The ethical aim of the Stoic comedian is to act like Demeter—to look Baubo in the face and to laugh. In architectural terms, it would be re-(up)righting as re-writing. Variously magnanimous, defiant, humorous, and vulnerable, two recent architectural projects evince such reconstruction of the "irreparable wound."

CEDARS SINAI COMPREHENSIVE CANCER CENTER, MORPHOSIS

Although entering at grade-level, patients in the Cedars Sinai Comprehensive Cancer Center must take their cancer down into a building with no ground at grade-level upon which to stand upright— a building that had to be built not on, but in, the ground (fig. 11). So just as patients turn left into the elevator to go down, Morphosis builds a window on the right, opening on to an architectural image of the patient's real world—a world of space, light, and the vault of heaven, but with no grade-level ground upon which to stand upright

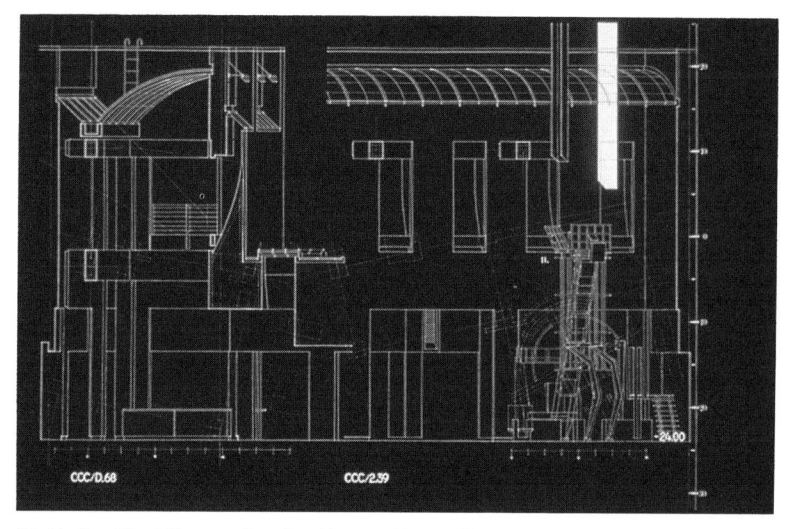

11. Cedars Sinai Comprehensive Cancer Center. Section drawing

(fig. 12). Opposite, a tree grows out of a box in the air at grade-level ground, if there were any. The construction returns the lack of ground as a construction of that lack. It re-presents absence as an architectural event upon the non-existent, but nonetheless insistent surface of the grade-level ground.

12. Window at grade-level to sculpture
13. Sculpture with jungle gym, video monitors, and aquarium

At the bottom of the elevator, a patient walks out of the elevator to see the tree's lack of ground-level as a sky-level that gives a new ground to stand on (fig. 13). The tree now has an appendage—roots—forming a jungle gym on a grade-level under ground. The construction returns the lack of ground as a double that reverses that lack.

DIVISIBLE BY TWO, JOHN WHITEMAN

John Whiteman's pavilion "Divisible By Two." plays the role of a four-sided "out-house" (fig. 14). On each side, a set of metal doors bears the signs: Damen and Herren (figs. 15 and 16).

14. "Divisible by Two." Pavilion. Elevation

The building was designed to explore the political power of architecture.[28] It re-constructs the insistent event of sexual difference upon the surface of bodies, where political power makes its impact. It reverses active and passive, constructing itself as surfaces that support its pipe frame. There is space to stand between the doors and the walls (fig. 17).

15-16. Door Details

The pavilion builds the event of the reversal of (sexual) difference itself. On the outside, the metal surfaces divide the sexes (fig. 18). Which door would you open? What do you expect to find inside? Inside there is only collapse—of *pharmakon*, of palinode, and of sexual difference itself. Inside there is no separation, but only more metal surfaces with no signs, each reflecting the other (figs. 19 and 20). The pavilion is "divisible by two" divisions.

17. Surfaces support the metal frame leaving walk space between
18. Exterior doors divide the sexes

The exterior offers the viewer a superficially Classical face of bi-univocal difference between the presence and absence of the phallus, a re-(up)righting of meaning as *sens unique*. But inside division is divided. Meaning is re-written as the counter-effectuation of difference in a single direction. Sexual difference is infinitely divided in both directions, in both senses at once. Not everyone laughs.

19. Interior reflecting surfaces
20. Interior without sexual division

Inside some musicians played a concert (fig. 21). On the outside one night someone wrote "Treason Architecture" and put a bomb inside. There was a rape, a "wound" I do not heal by re-writing it here (fig. 22).

21. Interior with musicians   22. Press reports of the bombing

1. My translation from G. Colli and M. Montinari, eds., "Preface to the Second Edition," vol. 3, *The Gay Science, Friedrich Nietzsche, Sämtliche Werke* (Berlin and New York: Walter de Gruyter, 1967-77), 352.
2. An "infinitival event"—see below, p. 118.
3. We know of Baubo mainly from the description of her role in the mythology of Demeter by two early Christian apologists: Clement of Alexandria, *Protrepticus* 2, 20, 1-21.1 and Arnobius Afer, *Adversus nationes* 5, 25 p.196, 3, ed. Reifferscheid (*Orphica Fragmenta* 52, ed. O. Kern). For Greek *xenia* "hospitality" as the exchanges of food, gifts, stories, (and women in legitimate marriage) that make the *xeinos* "stranger, guest" into a *philos* "one of one's own" or one who belongs to the same *oikos* "household," see E. Benveniste, *Le vocabulaire des institutions indo-européenes*, vol. 1 (Paris: Minuit, 1969), 335-53. In Greek thought, without *xenia* there can be no civilized human culture. Violations of the norm of *xenia*—such as Paris's abduction of Helen or the takeover of Odysseus's house and the attempted marriage of Penelope by the Suitors—are avenged by Zeus.
4. In the most popular form of the myth, recounted in the *Homeric Hymn to Demeter* (lines 90-300), the mourning of Demeter is dispelled verbally by one Iambe—an old woman from whose name is derived "iambic" blame poetry and "iambic" verse. By telling dirty jokes, Iambe makes the mourning goddess laugh and accept hospitality.
5. For Figure 1, see J. Millingen, "Baubo." *Annali dell'Instituto Archeologico*, Vol. 15 (1843), 72-97. The pig was sacred to Demeter: besides being sacrificed by each initiate, the pig was figured on the coins of Eleusis with the goddess herself on the reverse side, and terra-cotta images of the animal were often dedicated in her temples. In addition, the Greek noun *choiros*, "young pig, porker," bore an additional sense of "female genital" upon which the Comic poets liked to pun. The figurine is thus a visual version of the word's *double-entendre*. For Figure 2, see H. Winnefeld, "Das Heligtum der Demeter und Kore," in T. Wiegand and H. Schrader, *Priene. Ergebnisse*

der Ausgrabungen und Untersuchunger in der Jahren 1895-1898, (Berlin: 1904), 161. For the function of these figurines, we may compare the molded cakes of sesame and honey in the shape of female *ephebaia* "pubic region, pubic hair" carried by women celebrating the Thesmophoria (a festival of Demeter) throughout Sicily (see the report of the *Peri Thesmon* by Heraclides of Syracuse cited in Athenaeus, *Deipnosophistae*, 14, 647). The name of these cakes, *mulloi*, would appear to be cognate with the neuter noun *mullon* "lip" and the verb *mullo* "to grind," used to denote illicit intercourse (Eustathius 1885.22) and derived from *mule* "mill, lower millstone, hard formations in a woman's womb".

6. Plutarch, *Bravery of Women*, section 248, records an exemplary anecdote: when the warrior Bellerphon cursed the land of Lycia with sterility and moved against it with a tidal wave at his back, the men of the country could not deter him, but "the women, pulling up their dresses, went to meet him; and when he for shame retreated, the sea, it is said, retreated with him."

7. Sigmund Freud notes the existence of the Baubo myth and its apparent representation in the figurines from Priene in his paper, "A Mythological Parallel to a Visual Obsession" (1916), SE, XIV.337-338.

8. For the specifics of the analysis below, see A. Bergren, "Helen's 'Good Drug': *Odyssey* IV 1-305," *Contemporary Literary Hermeneutics and the Interpretation of Classical Texts*, ed. S. Kresic (Ottawa: University of Ottawa Press, 1981), 200-14.

9. *Odyssey* Book 4, lines 220-34: "Into the wine they were drinking, she cast a drug (*pharmakon*), grief-less, without anger, a forgetfulness of all sorrows. Whoever should drink it down, once it was mixed in the bowl, for that day would not drop a tear on his cheeks, not if his mother and father should die, not if men should slay with the bronze before him his brother or his own son, and with his eyes he should see it. Such were the crafty drugs (*pharmaka*) the daughter of Zeus possessed, good ones, given to her by the wife of Thon, Polydamna of Egypt, where the fertile earth bears the most drugs; many good in mixture and many wretched . . . Now when she put in the drug and ordered the wine to be poured, beginning again the stories (*mythoi*), she spoke."

10. See Ovid, *Metamorphoses*, Book 3, lines 322-38. For a complete analysis of this myth, see L. Brisson, *Le Mythe de Tirésias. Essai d'analyse structurale* (Leiden: Brill, 1976).

11. Compare G. Deleuze, "Platon et le simulacre" in *Logique de sens* (Paris: Éditions de Minuit, 1969), 293-8. The English translation, *The Logic of Sense*, trans. M. Lester (New York: Columbia University Press, 1990), 253-59, is quoted below with occasional alterations. See in particular p. 254: "Platonism is the philosophical *Odyssey* and the Platonic dialectic is neither a dialectic of contradiction nor of contrariety, but a dialectic of rivalry (*amphisbetesis*), a dialectic of rivals and suitors"; and 256: "Copies are secondary possessors. They are well-founded pretenders, guaranteed by resemblance; simulacra are like false pretenders, built upon a dissimilarity, implying an essential perversion or a deviation. It is in the sense that Plato divides in two the domain of images-idols: on one hand there are *copies-icons*, on the other *simulacra-phantasms*."

12. See e.g. *Timaeus* 30b4-5: "Having constructed (*sunistas:sun* "together, with" + *istas histemi* "make stand, set up") intelligence (*nous*) in the soul and the soul in the body, he built together (*sunetektaineto: sun* "together, with" + *tektaino* "build'" cf. *archi-tekton*) the totality (*to pan*)."

13. For the details of what follows, see Deleuze, *Logic of Sense* 1-11, 148-53 (*Logique du sens* 9-21, 174-79) and Michel Foucault, "Theatricum Philosophicum," in *Language, Counter-Memory, Practice: Selected Essays and Interviews*, trans. D. Bouchard and S. Simon (Ithaca: Cornell University Press, 1977).

14. French *insister*, translated in *Logic of Sense* as "subsist or inhere" (e.g., 5).

15. Compare Deleuze: "The only time of bodies and states of affairs is the present. For the living present is the temporal extension which accompanies the act, expresses

and measures the action of the agent and the passion of the patient. But to the degree that there is a unity of bodies among themselves, to the degree that there is a unity of active and passive principles, a cosmic present embraces the entire universe; only bodies exist in space, and only the present exists in time." *Logic of Sense*, 4 (13).

16. Compare Deleuze: "They [the incorporeal events] are not living presents but infinitives: the unlimited Aion, the becoming [*devenir*, the infinitive "to become"] which divides itself infinitely in past and future and always eludes the present. Thus time must be grasped twice, in two complementary though mutually exclusive fashions. First it must be grasped entirely as the living present in bodies which act and are acted upon. Second, it must be grasped entirely as an entity infinitely divisible into past and future, and into the incorporeal effects which result from bodies, their actions and their passions. Only the present exists in time and gathers together or absorbs the past and future. But only the past and future inhere [*insistent*] in time and divide each present infinitely. These are not three successive dimensions, but two simultaneous readings of time." *Logic of Sense*, 5 (14).

17. Deleuze gives the example of Alice: "Alice and *Through the Looking-Glass* involve a category of very special things: events, pure events. When I say 'Alice becomes larger,' I mean that she becomes larger than she was. By the same token, however, she becomes smaller than she is now. Certainly, she is not bigger and smaller at the same time. She is larger now; she was smaller before. But it is at the same moment that one becomes larger than one was and smaller than one becomes. This is the simultaneity of a becoming whose characteristic is to elude the present. Insofar as it eludes the present, becoming does not tolerate the separation or the distinction of before and after, or of past and future. It pertains to the essence of becoming to move and to pull in both directions [*sens*] at once: Alice does not grow without shrinking, and visa versa. Good sense [*le bon sens*] affirms that in all things there is a determinable sense of direction (*sens*); but paradox is the affirmation of both senses or directions at once . . . Paradox is initially that which destroys good sense as the only direction [*le bon sens comme sens unique*], but it is also that which destroys common sense [*le sens commun*] as the assignation of fixed identities." *Logic of Sense*, 1, 3 (9,12).

18. Deleuze quotes the Classical philosopher Emile Bréhier: "When the scalpel cuts through the flesh, the first body produces upon the second not a new property but a new attribute, that of being cut. The *attribute* does not designate any real *quality* . . . , it is, to the contrary, always expressed by the verb, which means that it is not a being, but a way of being . . . It is purely and simply a result, or an effect which is not to be classified among beings." *Logic of Sense* 5, (14). For the wound as the Stoic event *par excellence*, see 148-153, 211 (174-179, 246).

19. Deleuze explains: "Yet, what is more intimate or essential to bodies than events such as growing, becoming smaller, or being cut? What do the Stoics mean when they contrast the thickness of bodies with these incorporeal events which would play only on the surface, like a mist on the prairie (even less than a mist, since a mist is after all a body)? Mixtures are in bodies, and in the depth of bodies: a body penetrates another and coexists with it in all of its parts, like a drop of wine in the ocean, or fire in iron. One body withdraws from another, like liquid from a vase. Mixtures in general determine the quantitative and qualitative states of affairs: the dimensions of an ensemble—the red of iron, the green of a tree. But what we mean by 'to grow,' 'to diminish,' 'to become red,' 'to become green,' 'to cut' and 'to be cut,' etc., is something entirely different. These are no longer states of affairs—mixtures deep inside bodies—but incorporeal events at the surface which are the results of these mixtures." *Logic of Sense*, 5-6 (14-15).

20. Compare Deleuze: "Moreover, the Stoics are the first to reverse Platonism and to bring about a radical inversion. For if bodies with their states, qualities and quantities assume all the characteristics of substance and cause, conversely, the characteristics of the Idea [Form] are relegated to the other side, that is to the impassive extra-Being which is sterile, inefficacious, and on the surface of things: the

ideational or the incorporeal can no longer be anything other than an 'effect'... These are effects in the causal sense, but also sonorous, optical, or linguistic 'effects' —and even less, or much more, since they are no longer corporeal entities, but rather form the entire Idea. What was eluding the Idea climbed up to the surface, that is, the incorporeal limit, and represents now all possible *ideality*, the latter being stripped of its causal and spiritual efficacy." *Logic of Sense*, 7 (16-17).

21. Compare the case of Alice, as described by Deleuze: "In *Through the Looking Glass* ... events, differing radically from things, are no longer sought in the depths, but at the surface, in the faint incorporeal mist which escapes from bodies, a film without volume which envelops them, a mirror which reflects them, a chessboard on which they are organized according to plan. Alice is no longer able to make her way through the depths. Instead, she releases her incorporeal double... As a general rule, only little girls understand Stoicism; they have the sense of the event and release an incorporeal double." *Logic of Sense*, 9-10 (19-20).

22. Deleuze, *Logic of Sense*, 17-18 (8).

23. Compare Deleuze: "What does it mean then to will the event? Is it to accept war, wounds, and death when they occur? It is probable that resignation is only one more figure of *ressentiment*, since *ressentiment* has many figures ... [There is] a good deal of ignominy in saying that war concerns everybody, for this is not true. It does not concern those who use it or those who serve it—creatures of *ressentiment*. And there is as much ignominy in saying that everyone has his or her own war or particular wound, for this is not true of those who scratch at their sores—creatures of bitterness and *ressentiment*. It is true only of the free man, who grasps the event, and does not allow it to be effectuated without performing as actor its counter-effectuation." *Logic of Sense* 149, 152 (174, 178-79).

24. Deleuze, *Logic of Sense*, 149 (175).

25. Deleuze: "Why is every event a kind of plague, war, wound, or death? Is this simply to say that there are more unfortunate than fortunate events: No, this is not the case since the question here is about the double structure of every event ... Death has an extreme and definite relation to me and my body and is grounded in me, but it also has no relation to me at all—it is incorporeal and infinitive, impersonal, grounded only in itself. On one side, there is the part of the event which is realized and accomplished; on the other, there is the 'part of the event which cannot realize its accomplishment.' There are thus two accomplishments, which are like effectuation and counter-effectuation. It is in this way that death and its wound are not simply events among other events. Every event is like death, double and impersonal in its double. *Logic of Sense*, 151-52 (176). (The translation by M. Lester of *contre-effectuation* as 'counter-actualization' obscures the connection of the process with the event *as effect*.)

26. Deleuze, *Logic of Sense*, 151 (177).

27. Deleuze: "Only the free man, therefore, can comprehend all violence in a single act of violence, and every mortal event *in a single Event* which no longer makes room for the accident, and which denounces and deposes the power of *ressentiment* within the individual as well as the power within society. It is by propagating *ressentiment* that the tyrant makes himself allies, namely slaves and servants. Only the revolutionary is free from the *ressentiment* by which one always participates in and profits from an oppressive order. *But one and the same Event?* ... It is at this mobile and precise point, where all events are thus reunited in one that transmutation is produced: the point where death is returned against death, where to die [*le mourir*] is to dismiss death from office [*comme la destitution de la mort*], where the impersonality of dying no longer marks only the moment when I lose myself outside of myself, but the moment when death loses itself in itself and the figure that the most singular life takes in order to substitute itself for me." *Logic of Sense*, 152 (179).

28. See J. Whiteman, *Divisible by Two* (Cambridge: CIAU/MIT Press, 1990).

MARY PEPCHINSKI

THE LANDSCAPE OF MEMORY

Germany and Berlin are the ultimate modern places. Earning them this distinction are the relative frequency and the ferocious intensity with which politics, economics, militarism, and social forces have changed this society's built and natural environments. Architectural production, building preservation and destruction, city planning, as well as the radical alterations performed by non-architects (the Wall, bombed-out cities) were and continue to be the primary means of expressing national and local fluctuations in character. Despite current changes, prior manipulations of the built environment remain as both visible and invisible witnesses to the passage of time, and as proof of an increasingly complex urban and national context.

The roles of a European capital city are to mirror and to encapsulate a country. The terms "prewar," "postwar," and "post-unification" historically situate Germany and accurately describe distinct Berlins: prewar Berlin—unified, modern, "the German Chicago," site of political conflicts, magnet for radical culture; postwar Berlin—divided, ruined, rebuilt, a place of memories, superpower confrontations (the airlift of 1947–48), political and social unrest (East Berlin in 1953 and 1989; West Berlin in 1968); and post-unification Berlin—still to be defined, city of the immediate future. In each phase, Berlin offers a precise reflection of contemporary Germany.

Bismarck united the German princely states into the German Reich in 1871, making it a latecomer to modern statehood. After defeat in the First World War and during the liberal Weimar Republic Berlin was a magnet for radical culture, a natural stopping point for artists travelling across Europe. Between 1933 and 1945 the German fascist state was controlled by Adolf Hitler and the National Socialists who developed plans to transform Berlin into "Germania," a city of 10 million and capital of the world. At the end of the Second World War in 1945 Berlin and a substantial part of Germany were reduced to ruins. Following defeat by the Allies Germany's borders were redefined and the country was divided into zones of Soviet (East) and Allied (West) occupation; these later evolved into the German Democratic Republic and the Federal Republic of Germany. Berlin, located in the Soviet Zone, retained the status of a jointly occupied city (American, French, British, and Soviet).[1] Between 1961 and 1989 the east-west division of Germany was deliberately manifest by the "Iron Curtain." In Berlin it was physically manifest by the Wall.

During modernism's early years Germany commissioned more modern architecture than any other country and was home to the Bauhaus's influential and pioneering pedagogy. From 1910 to approximately 1933 the German capital city supported a vibrant, locally based architectural community. Around 1910 Peter Behrens's Berlin office employed Mies van der Rohe, Walter Gropius, and Jeanneret (Le Corbusier); by the late 1920s prominent local architects included Max and Bruno Taut, Lily Reich, Erich Mendelsohn, and Hans Scharoun, to name but a few.[2]

Julius Posener has remarked that unlike that in Paris in the 1920s, modern architecture in Berlin was a reality.[3] A supportive liberal government encouraged the construction of new housing and the preservation of existing forests, creating a permanent green belt around the city.[4] By the end of the twenties a vast number of building types including housing, theaters, cinemas, factories, department stores, recreational centers, office buildings, and even political memorials had been constructed in the modern idiom. After 1933 the Nazis vigorously censored all forms of modern art and focussed attention in Berlin on realizing large public buildings to serve their political goals.[5] By 1940 many modernist practitioners had either left the country or ceased working.[6]

Immediately after the war Roberto Rossellini made a film describing Berlin, *Germania: Anno Zero* (Germany, Year One). The title is a precise evocation of the late 1940s when, out of chaos and destruction, Germany began to create for itself a physical, political, social, and cultural identity. Architecture, preservation, and urban planning played vital roles in this reconstruction.

After 1945, thirty percent of the population was homeless. Housing became a priority, and some new residential buildings were blatantly ideological. In 1951 East Berlin authorities began the

Stalinallee (now the Karl Marx Allee), a monumental neobaroque boulevard planned as the "first socialist street on German soil."[7] In 1957 West Berlin opened the Hansaviertel; this centerpiece of the "Interbau" exhibition, a freely organized collection of modern towers, slabs, and low-rise buildings designed by a coterie of European and American architects, was intended to demonstrate "the strengths of the technology and design of the Free World in all the variety of their forms."[8]

The division of the city is also conspicuous in postwar institutional architecture, which reflects either an inheritance (East Berlin) or a lack (West Berlin). In the past decade East Berlin has been restoring eighteenth- and nineteenth-century neoclassical public buildings along Unter Den Linden, the Platz der Akademie, and the Museumsinsel. In the fifties, West Berlin began constructing new institutions such as the Free University in Dahlem (Candelis, Josic, Woods, 1963–73), the Culture Forum (Mies and Scharoun, 1960–present), the Congress Hall in the Tiergarten (Stubbins, 1957), and the American Memorial Library in Kreuzberg (Bornemann, Kreuer, Jobst, Wille, 1954). This rapid postwar institutional rebuilding should not be viewed merely as a cultural effort; it was also directly influenced by postwar American foreign policy. Realized during the burgeoning *Wirtschaftswunder* of the 1950s, many of these projects received financial (and at times technical) support from the Ford and the Benjamin Franklin Foundations, prominent American organizations.

Finally, there is the *Sanierung*, meaning renovation or rehabilitation and deriving from the Latin *sanare*, to cure.[9] Initially this involved removal of extensive rubble and debris, followed by repairs to existing infrastructure and the removal of buildings deemed not worth saving. An additional nationwide rehabilitation process was aimed at erasing the traces of Hitler's fascist state. This included the early and rapid destruction of certain Nazi buildings (e.g.the Gestapo Headquarters at Prinz Albrecht Palais) and the elimination of propaganda and artifacts associated with the period of National Socialism (renaming streets named after Hitler and Goebbels, removing placards and posters, etc.).[10] Forty years after the war numerous buildings and objects from the National Socialist period remain. Although attempts to transform or remake this legacy have been required of professionals and bureaucrats, the task often has proven paralysing and the results unsatisfactory.[11]

In contrast to the official buildings and sanctioned building programs stands another layer of Berlin: an *architecture of memory*. Memory is sheltered either unintentionally in monuments created by the chance survival of buildings, artifacts, and spaces, or willfully preserved through conscious individual or collective actions. This aspect of the physical environment is significant for two reasons. First, it can offer a direct critique of the social, political and architectural policies that continue to shape postwar Berlin. Second, it can allow ideas about architecture and the urban landscape to exist outside of official policy to create a new urban vernacular.

Among the numerous inadvertent urban memorials are subway lines originating in the west and speedily bypassing the east through closed stations guarded by the occasional soldier and dog; singular tenements, standing like beached whales, surrounded by now vacant yet once dense urban fabric; the Oranienburger Straße Synagogue, Berlin's main house of Jewish worship, attacked on the Reichkristallnacht, unused and in ruin; a lone allee of trees in a sprawling unpaved open field, the sole marker of Potsdamer Straße, prewar Berlin's "Broadway." Among the forms of deliberate preservation is personal recollection, ironic in its invisibility. This *architecture of memory* is aptly illustrated by Wim Wenders and Peter Handke's film *Der Himmel Über Berlin*: an old man leaves Scharoun's State Library in search of Potsdamer Platz. Arriving at the site he finds a mud field, an allee of trees, and, along the eastern border, the Wall. "Imagination is memory,"[12] noted James Joyce and, for the old man, the Platz is alive with traffic, people, and shops existing in his imagination. In this scene Wenders and Handke describe the two aspects of Berlin's contemporary reality—its present physical condition and the living memory of its former presence.

A more publicly visible mode of personal recollection is the use of the written word to stimulate the act of remembering, or, more simply, to declare facts. Most poignant are the inscriptions found in the now overgrown and untended Weißensee cemetery, the major burial ground of the city's prewar Jewish community. On the gravestones one can read 200-year-long family sagas. The most recent inscriptions have been added by survivors of the Holocaust—"Murdered at Auschwitz," "Murdered at Theresienstadt," "emigrated and died in Lima," or "deceased in New York."

Many non-architects have actively shaped West Berlin's present form. One prominent example is *public outcry*, which saved the bombarded ruin of the Kaiser Wilhelm Memorial Church slated by the Senat of West Berlin for demolition in the early fifties. Public action provoked a critical act of preservation saving the disfigured shell as a somber and emotional reminder of the recent past, demanding it become the new heart of Berlin.[13] Similar, sometimes spontaneous, critical efforts were directed at the Wall: graffiti, posters, paintings, and performances transformed an instrument of inhumanity into a collective measure of conscience.

In *The Architecture of the City*, Aldo Rossi interpreted the classical idea of buildings and objects containing or inspiring memory as a broad construct to describe the collectivity of meaning embedded in a city:

One can say that the city itself is the collective memory of the people, and like memory it is associated with objects and places. The city is the locus of the collective memory. This relationship between the locus and the citizenry then becomes the city's prominent image, both of architecture and of landscape and as certain artifacts become part of its memory, new ones emerge. In this entirely positive sense great ideas flow through the history of the city and give shape to it.[14]

Berlin, with its accidental and deliberate monuments, can be seen as a repository of the collective and conflicted memory of contemporary Germany. Yet compared to the seen and unseen fragments of the Rome of Rossi's investigations, those constituting Berlin's example are more immediate. Many Berliners still recall a city whole and unruined, have lived through its division, and have witnessed its reunification.

In recent decades, West Berlin had become an ironic Großstadt: the largest city of the Federal Republic of Germany, it was in reality a political, cultural, and geographic island. By present West German standards it was poor, supported by infusions of capital from the United States (the Marshall Plan) and the German Federal Republic. As part of this subsidization policy the West Berlin Senate increasingly invited foreign architects to participate in open and limited competitions for building commissions in the city. The resulting architecture had begun to lend West Berlin a distinct postwar identity as an architectural spectacle.

The largest organized effort has been West Berlin's International Building Exhibition (IBA), which closed in 1987 on the city's 750th birthday. The eight-year-long IBA instigated myriad housing projects by some of the best known contemporary architects in several Berlin neighborhoods—from former inner-city areas by the Wall to more suburban, parklike sites—as well as several institutional buildings.

The involvement of foreign architects became IBA's *raison d'etre*. As Kurt Andersen noted, the IBA "would be unremarkable without its world-class aesthetic aspirations" the many winners of its competitions constituting "a sort of international who's who" of the architectural world.[15] Yet such international aspirations are not peculiar to IBA, or to West Berlin. In the late twentieth century the combined effects of mass communications, global transportation, and what Paul Ricouer has identified as "the phenomenon of universalization" have added a new dimension to the production, execution, and reception of architecture worldwide.[16]

In its published catalogues the IBA associated itself with the history of nineteenth- and twentieth-century architectural exhibitions such as Weißenhof Siedlung (Stuttgart, 1927) and Hansaviertel (West Berlin, 1957), where seminal urban and architectural experiments had been realized at full scale.[17] The IBA, however, broke from the tradition of temporary or physically isolated exhibition structures, commissioning permanent buildings for existing neighborhoods. The question of context instead confronted the IBA architects: What is intrinsic to a city, site, or place? What is "Berlinness?"

The contemporary character of Berlin reveals its origin as many small, distinct villages. Different parts of the city—eighteenth-century gridded urban extensions, nineteenth-century garden suburbs, early twentieth-century and postwar Siedlungen—express its variegated past. This collage was intensified by unsystematic postwar planning and building strategies, as well as the violent urban rupturing produced by the East-West division, that further contributed to the city's irregular character and multitextured urban fabric. Berlin's context derived from the juxtaposition of old and new, names of former streets and surviving places, the fragile encircling tension of the Wall, and, finally, memories. As Walter Benjamin writes of his Paris walks, a city's inner life is unleashed through encounters with details of place and nuances of street life:

> Not to find one's way in a city may well be uninteresting and banal. It requires ignorance—nothing more. But to loose oneself in a city—as one looses oneself in a forest—that calls for quite a different schooling. Then signboards and street names, passers-by, roofs, kiosks or bars must speak to the wanderer like a crackling twig under his feet in the forest, like the startling call of a bittern in the distance, like the sudden stillness of a clearing with a lily standing erect at its center.[18]

Because of its composite qualities the essence of Berlin is particularly difficult to grasp, and mere repetition of physical details (an effort to reproduce "Berlinness" through its reduction to material or style) has been an arbitrary but common design strategy. A number of the IBA participants chose to lend their architecture local character by drawing upon the city's nineteenth-century public and industrial buildings (red and gold brickwork, painted steel detailing); others found recourse in turn-of-the-century *Mietskaseren* (muted stucco facade colorings, regular, repeated fenestration, pronounced entries to interior courtyards, emphatic towerlike corners). Still others emulated specific works of past architectural masters such as Schinkel or the various radical experimenters of the early twentieth century. Meditations on structures unique to Berlin—the Wall being the most prominent—were the basis for a series of generative geometric or spatial operations. Most successful were buildings able to convey the meaning inherent in a given site or its immediate surroundings through spatial means.

The IBA had little direct power to commission architects. Rather it functioned like a planning and public relations office for architecture with a fifty-million-dollar budget used to organize competitions, symposia, and exhibitions and to publish catalogues. Competition winners were joined to local developers charged with constructing designs according to the established West German standards for social housing. Thus, the IBA effectively divided the architectural design process: it required a *design* architect responsible for an idea and schematic design concept and a *contact* architect whose job it was to produce contract documents, attend meetings, and supervise construction. This form of collaborative and cross-cultural practice has outlasted the formal tenure of IBA, challenging conventionally accepted notions that the work of architecture must be born solely from the hand of one designer and his/her design office. (Despite this division of labor, the *design* architect continues to be viewed as the main author of a project.) It is also rapidly becoming a normative condition for many (not only West Berlin) architects, such as those commissioned to build in diverse locations or those fiscally unable to maintain a permanent in-house staff.

In 1984 IBA Director Josef Paul Kleihues claimed that the value of "outsiders" lay in their capacity to "provide necessary criticism of routine" and to overcome a "prevailing instrumental rationality." He continued: "We need provocative theories and artistic stimulus. We need these as a critical impulse for our competitions, for our seminars, for our exhibitions, for the International Building Exhibition as a whole."[19] Indeed, IBA made the city an extremely interesting place, particularly for students. It increased public awareness of contemporary architecture and aroused public curiosity about the many new structures. Yet, despite theoretical claims to the contrary, IBA departed from the example of past exhibitions where the mass public experience of new architecture was presumed vital and necessary.[20] With the exception of some tours given in the IBA's final year very few people—professional and lay public—have been able to confront this new urban architecture. Except for the press, most people can only experience the IBA structures from the exterior. The public's virtual isolation from the IBA buildings was particularly ironic in West Berlin. Due to a physically isolated situation, West Berliners were avid museum-goers and event enthusiasts—the weekend ritual of *Spazierengehen* remained strong. Had IBA encouraged involvement on the part of the public its local success would have undoubtedly been much enhanced. To compensate for the lack of access, however, the IBA went directly to the mass media to disseminate its work.

Images of West Berlin's new architecture are ubiquitous: they can be found in IBA's own catalogues, professional and popular journals, newspapers, history books, museums, and galleries. The potential for publication has consequences for architectural design. Pierre-Alain Croset noted how two influences on architectural magazines, aesthetic models created by advertising and an increasingly "fragmented and unfocused" act of reading, have encouraged the production of architecture that tends to be "spectacular." Croset described how this situation, combined with an attitude that devalues descriptions addressing the spatial aspects of architecture, has fostered "the present tendency of architects to underrate the problems tied to the spatial experience of the building while paying excessive attention to the external visual character of the object."[21]

Mass produced photographs take on a life of their own; as Susan Sontag has written, "cameras define reality. The production of images also furnishes a ruling ideology."[22] The extensive mass-media and photographic coverage of IBA constitute part of West Berlin's official image. They declare the uniqueness of the city, its cosmopolitan status. Images describe a city that erects not mere public housing but *extraordinary* public housing. Yet this highly selective view is not complete. To cite Sontag, "Photography implies that we know about the world if we accept it as the camera records it. But this is the opposite of understanding, which starts from *not* accepting the world as it looks."[23] Only by rejecting this singular, exclusive impression can other faces and modalities of Berlin begin to appear.

The West Berlin of today is a densely layered text. Seventy years ago Berlin's export to the world was the example of a vital architectural culture of place; its modern structures influenced significant architectural developments of this century. Today West Berlin markets a model for architectural production; new buildings there substantially impact methods of local and international practice. Described by Vittorio Magnagno Lampugnani as the "IBA effect," Berlin's government-supported architecture can be imported and commodified. While it may enhance the city's image at a global scale, it can impact unevenly on local experience.[24] The "IBA effect" also underscores the fact that some historians believe that neither West Berlin nor West Germany have produced—or would have been able to produce—any internationally recognized architects in the post-war genaration.[25]

If many IBA architects were prevented from exploring the historic or mythic dimensions of place this was due in part to implications suggested by the organization's directives. Specifically, in the Southern Friedrichstadt portion of Kreuzberg, the IBA insisted upon reusing the existing 18th century street pattern and its corresponding perimeter block form. Resulting IBA infill structures evoke "normal" urban growth within a formerly fragmented city fabric, potentially leading to a misreading of the city as having naturally evolved into its present state. With the exception of a few projects, a major aspect of Berlin's history—the deformation caused by cataclysmic destruction—has been rendered invisible.

Certain of the IBA commissions and projects located in the Südliche Friedrichstadt area of Kreuzberg near Checkpoint Charlie were informed by aspects of the architecture of memory and its symbolic importance: the Office of Metropolitan Architecture's unbuilt planning and housing proposals, a proposed through-block "street" with housing by Berlin architects Klaus-Theo Brenner and Benedict Tonon, and John Hejduk's built tower and two low housing wings as well as his unexecuted plan for the area. These projects do not hide the torn and fragmented urban landscape, nor do they try to improve, cure, or solve the extant conditions by adhering to the officially prescribed IBA master plan, which called for rebuilding the prewar perimeter block.

In these projects architecture opens up and refers spatially to the ruins. The past is not hidden from but rather drawn into conversation with the present. Through this work one can begin to understand the condition of architecture in Berlin today, to feel the tension created by the superimposition of an official, controlled, building program and an unofficial, spontaneous, urban landscape. One facade, rife with contradictions, is displayed through the media as real. The other, lying beyond the borders of traditional architectural discourse, defies exploitation. One is left wondering, what can architecture offer?

Question: In your childhood did you come across people who talked critically of Adolf Hitler, Nazism and the final victory, or who told political jokes? Christa Wolf: Not one, not a single one! That was precisely the point! I never met one.[26]

On a recent early evening walk on the Teufelsberg[27] with an English speaking friend we found ourselves suddenly encircled by four young, gesticulating, leather-clad skinheads who accosted us with screams of "Deutschland, Deutschland, Ausländer raus! Ausländer raus!" (Germany, Germany, foreigners out! Foreigners out!) We made it to the hilltop and amidst a small crowd gathered to watch the sunset, pretended to ignore yet a larger group who strained their voices and threw up their arms to the sky chanting "Sieg Heil! Sieg

Heil!" Our terror began to subside after a few hours, giving way to disbelief and later pity. I desperately wanted to rationalize the evening as one spoiled by some aggressive, arrogant, and ultimately harmless young men. The knowledge that my strong desire to dismiss the event echoed the sensibility of so many others in the early 1930s when confronted by Hitler's Brown Shirts was deeply frightening.

"What is past is not dead; it is not even past. We cut ourselves off from it; we pretend to be strangers." So begins Christa Wolf's *A Model Childhood*, a fictionalized account of her youth in Nazi Germany.[28] In contemporary Germany the past continues to inhabit the present. Civil-service questionnaires still inquire if job applicants were persecuted under National Socialism; Allied and Soviet troops continue to occupy the country; personal photo albums preserve images of relatives in full military dress. Living with these still vital artifacts of a not so distant past is difficult and uncomfortable. As Walter Abish so bluntly expressed at the end of *How German Is It*, this situation produces revelations at once unwelcome and troubling for many. In an emotion-filled moment when Abish's protagonist realizes he is not the son of a oft viewed hero who had tried to murder Hitler but is in fact a bastard who could have been sired by any man between 1940 and 1945, he comes out of a trance in his doctor's office, his right arm held high in a stiff salute. Abish concludes, "Is it possible for anyone in Germany, nowadays, to raise his right hand, for whatever reasons, and not be flooded by the memory of a dream to end all dreams?"[29]

In the past decade there has been a growing cultural, social, and political awareness of the need to come to terms with the legacy of German fascism. Increasingly the mass media, cultural and educational institutions, citizens' groups, and professional organizations have explored the specific relationship of the National Socialist period to the present. It is in this atmosphere that many local governments have begun to sponsor open and limited competitions giving artists and architects the opportunity to propose memorials for resonant locations throughout the country—among them sites of former synagogues and places of deportation.

The traditional memorial has proved an inappropriate anachronism for confronting this troubled past. As one West Berlin critic noted in a review of a 1988 exhibition of commemorative projects:

In our time, memorials and monuments have become alien, hardly imaginable as the obligatory aesthetic standard for the representation of historical events and the state of political affairs. Either the breadth of public consensus is missing, or there is a shortage of collective understanding; yet for the effect of a memorial, both are indispensable.[30]

In his view, the most successful exhibited projects were those able to "stress the meaning of a site, leaving it substantially untouched." Yet emphasizing the significance of site—something that is frequently already evident or understood—is in itself insufficient.

It is difficult to claim that a single object, building, sound or sight can excite memory and stimulate an experience of emotional catharsis. Yet, often, encounters with the familiar and unremarkable bring to the surface what for long has been hidden or denied. To remember is not to witness passively, but to commemorate actively. Such action is often strikingly ordinary; one is reminded of the flowers, letters, and objects left spontaneously at the Vietnam Veterans Memorial in Washington D.C., the flowers and photographs placed on particular bunks at Theresienstadt, and the guest book note of a Holocaust survivor in Budapest's Dohány Street Synagogue, inscribed in fulfillment of a death-camp promise. A memorial that is neither anachronistic nor alienating must indeed call out the inherent meaning of a site, but it should also awaken the potential of the ordinary and familiar to engender meaning that is collectively rather than selectively understood.

The American, made-for-T.V. film "Holocaust," which aired on West German television (Z.D.F) in 1979, accomplished this feat. To elucidate the film's impact Andreas Huyssen cites a thesis advanced by Alexander and Margarethe Mitscherlich that the greatest collective problem facing contemporary German society is the inability to confront and mourn the inherited guilt from the Holocaust. Explaining the power of this film in Germany, Huyssen noted that a number of factors converged to make *identification* with the assimilated German-Jewish protagonists possible.[31] Upon viewing the film, a mass audience was finally able to feel grief and mourn at the protagonists untimely deaths. Unlike previous German language avant-garde dramas (*The Investigation* by Peter Weiss; *The Deputy* by Rolf Hochhuth; *Andorra* by Max Frisch), which failed to provide identification and thus prevented an outpouring of emotion, the American-made movie addressed the real need of German society to engage in mourning. The result was a brief, collective catharsis echoing throughout Germany.

Huyssen's essay suggests the existence of an untapped and overlooked power residing in the ordinary and the familiar that could provide a basis for confronting the conflicting reality of contemporary Germany. Despite a working approach and sound intentions of architecture, one must still wonder what it can hope to accomplish there. The current architectural climate, represented by the IBA projects in Berlin (housing, urban design, and institutions) and by postwar building throughout West Germany (museums in particular), displays a fascination for new ideas. This demand is both enriching and disturbing. On one hand, Berlin's architecture of memory shows us that the buildings, spaces, and cities we inhabit offer more than shelter and specific private or public functions; they also embody emotion and meaning and mirror the "collective memory of a people." On the other hand, in much of the new, officially sponsored building the spatially evocative powers of architecture have been lost, at times replaced by indirect experience through the media. The results are a denial of the history and collective mythology of a site and a growing sense of placelessness.

To achieve what "Holocaust" did a decade ago—a collective catharsis beginning with individual reactions and magnifying, through multiplication, to society as a whole—I have been forced to work *outside* traditional parameters. The architecture of memory and a reaction to the prevailing climate of production inform projects that are not pure architecture, but a synthesis of art, landscape, and architecture. This fusion permits invention, but more importantly it calls for engaged personal experience for the emotional release caused by direct confrontation with the past.

Two Memorials

At Bahnhof Grunewald, West Berlin, the awareness of memory could be initiated by the collective voices and completed by the emotional recollections of each visitor. The project cannot be understood at a distance, nor does it function in the abstract; photographs reveal nothing of its essence. At Börneplatz, Frankfurt, the experience is similarly individual and collective. The ritual of graveside planting is transformed through repeated personal acts into a mass action intended to serve as a measure of conscience. Demanding engagement, both memorials speak to the commodified condition of contemporary building to engender an architecture that forces the creation of culture, not merely consumption of it.

A Memorial at Bahnhof Grunewald, West Berlin

Bahnhof Grunewald is a local West Berlin train station that was used to deport 50,000 Jews between 1941 and 1945. The memorial calls to mind the role it played during those years.

Grunewald is a wealthy residential neighborhood located on the edge of an extensive urban park. Relatively untouched by the bombings of World War II, it is composed today of villas, free-standing buildings, trees, and gardens. The serenity of the neighborhood clashes with the

THE LANDSCAPE OF MEMORY

STIMMEN IM TUNNEL
Dieses Denkmal fragt:
Da die Einwohner von Grunewald in der Zeit von 1941 bis 1945 fünfzigtausend Juden, die von Bahnhof Grunewald deportiert wurden "nicht gesehen" haben, werden sie heute ein Denkmal für diese gemordeten Juden bemerken?

STIMMEN IM TUNNEL: This Memorial asks: If, between 1941 and 1945, the residents of Grunewald did not see 50,000 Jews being deported, will they notice a memorial for these murdered people?

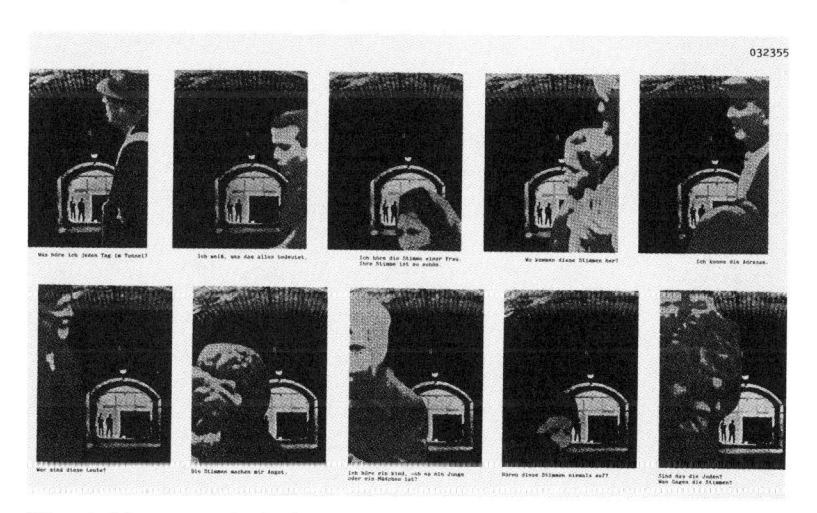

What do I hear every day in the tunnel?
I know, what all this means.
I hear the voice of a woman. Her voice is so beautiful.
Where do these voices come from?
I know the address.
Who are these people?
The voices make me scared.
I hear a child. It is a boy or a girl?
Will these voices never stop?
Are these the Jews? What are these voices saying?

139

image of thousands being packed into cattle cars and transported to a mysterious destination in the "East." If, from 1941 to 1945, the Grunewald residents did not *see* 50,000 fellow Jewish citizens being deported, will they *see* a memorial for these murdered people?

My design concept was simple: a memorial one can hear but not see. I proposed placing a double row of speakers in the station's long pedestrian tunnel. Each would softly resound with a different voice (an old woman, a child, a young man, etc.). The voices would belong to members of the surviving Jewish community of East and West Berlin. They would each read the deportation lists—names, ages, and addresses of Jews as well as the exact dates of their deportation. The street names would recall that a divided city had once been whole; the dates would create the aura of a fragment of time.

Walking though this memorial would be an experience of the imagination, a theater of the mind. For the average Berliner, the awareness of memory would be initiated by the voices but completed by the imagination.

A MEMORIAL AT BÖRNEPLATZ, FRANKFURT AM MAIN

The Börneplatz competition called for a public memorial in the heart of Frankfurt to commemorate the annihilation of the city's Jewish community. The proposed site, a portion of the former Börneplatz, is located at one corner of the old Jewish cemetery.

Jewish and Christian communities had long coexisted in Frankfurt. In the twelfth century the Jews built a synagogue near the Christian cathedral and defined the boundaries of their burial ground. As the city grew, it encircled the walled cemetery that, like a cathedral, a city wall, or a bridge, still served as a physical and cartographic point of orientation.

Today Frankfurt's Jewish community exists in diminished numbers. The former main Synagogue (once situated adjacent to the cemetery) was destroyed during the Reichskristallnacht of 1938. The platz surrounding the Synagogue, formerly named Börneplatz after a distinguished Jewish citizen of Frankfurt, has since the end of World War II been renamed Dominikanerplatz, after a nearby cloister.

Christianity and Judaism share a religious foundation in the Old Testament, where the first story concerning knowledge and loss is metaphorically told against the backdrop of a garden, the place of Paradise. My Börneplatz memorial also takes the form of a garden, a reminder of common roots.

Slightly raised on a stone base, the garden is entered by a set of stairs opposite the new entrance to the cemetery. Surrounding the

THE LANDSCAPE OF MEMORY

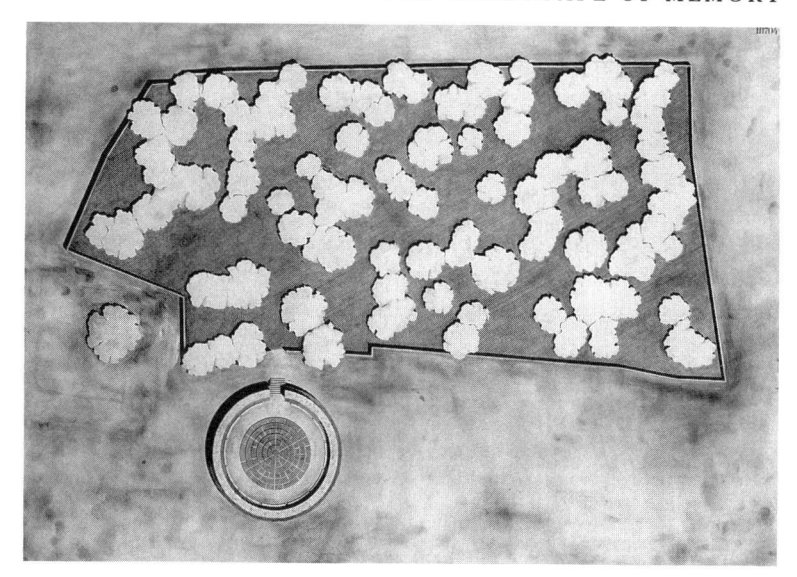

A Memorial at Börneplatz, site plan

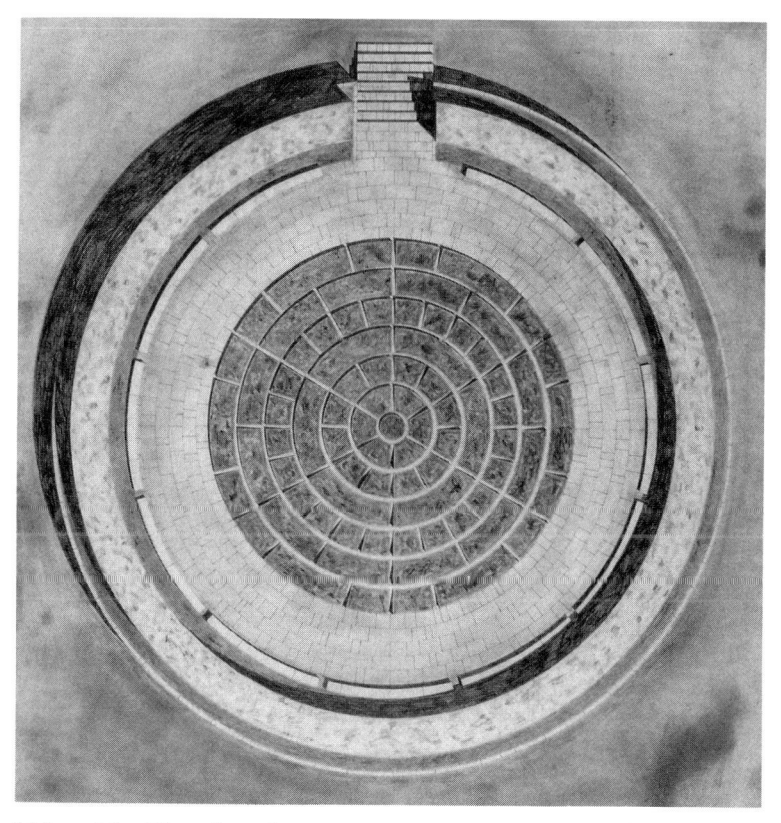

A Memorial at Börneplatz, plan

garden is a high hedge and, on the interior, a circle of low, stone benches. Seven concentric terraces, stacked like a round stepped pyramid, form the garden proper. Walking around the terraces, one is able to view the various plantings; seated on the surrounding stone benches, one can reflect in and upon this memorial.

The garden is both metaphor and symbol: a garden, like memory, requires nurturing, and the quality of care reflects the quality of memory. Vested with the power to create a garden either vital (well tended) or foul (forgotten), the citizens of Frankfurt can express and be witness to the state of their memory—direct and inherited—of Jewish persecution and annihilation.

A personal, even an emotional connection with the past would grow out of visiting and viewing this memorial. Thus the surrounding stone benches offer a place for visitors to sit, pause, reflect, rest, and look at one another across the garden.

As in most memorials, the object here is to arouse memory. Dedicated to the victims, it is ultimately aimed at the survivors, the people who remain long after the tragedy has ended. Looking across the garden, the question to those who use this garden simply as a quiet and passive place, is: If we or our ancestors had been more like Christians to one another, would the unthinkable have occurred?

POSTSCRIPT

This essay was begun in 1988 and completed in 1990. On November 9, 1989 East German citizens were allowed to travel freely to West Germany and West Berlin. Within days innumerable new border crossings were opened. In the coming decade, increasing contact between the former Bundesrepublik Deutschland and the former German Democratic Republic, implementation of German unification and monetary reform, the growing impact of the *Aussiedler* and the *Übersiedler*, a critical need for new housing, and the opening of the European Community in 1992 will impact on German cultural identity—and on architecture. The directions taken will be further complicated by lingering national ambivalence to the legacy of German fascism. One period of transformation has ended and another begun.

THE LANDSCAPE OF MEMORY

Removing the Wall at Potsdamer Platz to create a new border crossing, November, 1989

PEPCHINSKI

1. The subsequent naming of the Soviet sector as *Hauptstadt* of the German Democratic Republic violates an agreement stating that Berlin is not to resume its status as capital city.
2. Mies van der Rohe and Walter Gropius were still at work in Berlin during the 1920s, as were other well known architects such as the Luckhardt brothers, Martin Wagner, Ludwig Hilberseimer, and Hans Poelzig.
3. Comments given by Julius Posener on the opening of the exhibition "Berlin: 750 Years of Architecture" at the New National Gallery, West Berlin (May 1987).
4. Ronald Wiedenhoeft, "Workers Housing as Social Politics," *Culture and the Social Vision*, vol. IV of *VIA*, Journal of the Graduate School of Fine Arts, University of Pennsylvania (Philadelphia: Univ. of PA Press, 1980): 112-125.
5. Benjamin Warner, "Berlin—The Nomadic Homeland and the Corruption of Urban Spectacle" in *AD Profile: Post-war Berlin, An Architectural History*, ed. Doug Clelland (1982): 176
6. John Willets, *Art and Politics in the Weimar Period* (Pantheon: New York, 1978), 221.
7. Based on an account by a team led by Karolus Heil, "1945: The Second Destruction," *The Architectural Review* (April 1987): 38/4. The quote is changed to read "On 3rd February 1952 the foundation stone was laid for the revised designs for the first socialist street in Berlin" in Christian Borngräber, "Residential Buildings in Stalinallee," *AD Profile: Post-war Berlin, An Architectural History*, ed. Doug Clelland (1982): 36.
8. For a discussion of the Stalinallee see Karolus Heil, "750 Years of Berlin" in "Berlin: Origins to I.B.A.," *The Architectural Review* no.1082 (April 1987): 38. On Hansaviertel, see V.M. Lampugnani, "Architectural Exhibitions: A Fragmentary Historical Survey for Europe and the U.S.A." in *Schriftenreihe zur Internationalen Bauausstellung Berlin 1984–Die Neubaugebiete Projekte-Heft 2*, ed. Josef Paul Kleihues (Berlin: Quadriga GmbH Verlagsbuchhandlung KG, 1981), 54.
9. Herbert Lachmeyer, "Berlin: Die Verteilte Stadt" (Berlin: The Distributed City) in *Post-War Berlin*, 78-81.
10. The architecture of the National Socialist period presents a paradox. Recent scholarship has unearthed Hitler and Speer's ideology of construction, which mandated buildings be of stone (without structural steel) to insure that in a millennium the architecture would appear like the ruins of classical antiquity. A predicament arises: to let these structures fall into ruin can be seen as fulfilling the fascist's intentions; to destroy them outright can be seen as a cure rooted in denial; restoration and repair suggest an attempt to glorify the past. See Falk Jaeger, "Architektur Strafen und Geschichte Meinen," *Der Tagesspiegel*, (Oct. 6, 1989)
11. See Mary Pepchinski, "Berlin Academy of Science Competition and Controversy" *Progressive Architecture* (June, 1988): 27-29.
12. Brenda Maddox, *Nora: A Bibliography of Nora Joyce* (London: Minerva Paperback/Octapus Publishing, 1989), 4.
13. Wulf Schirmer, *Egon Eiermann* (Stuttgart: Deutsche Verlags-Anstalt GmbH, 1984), 164.
14. Aldo Rossi *The Architecture of the City* (Cambridge: MIT Press, 1982), 130.
15. Kurt Andersen, "Rebuilding Berlin—Yet Again," *TIME* (June 15, 1987): 66-68.
16. Many essays in a recent anthology edited by Beatriz Colomina demonstrate the impact of mechanical reproduction on architecture. Colomina notes how photography has greatly increased the architectural audience to include not only users but tourists, readers of journals, clients, exhibition viewers, etc. Extending this observation, I would argue that photography has also substantially effected the architect, who now has access to an expanded field for the dissemination of ideas and realization of projects. Further, photography and the broad reach of the media render formerly restrictive distinctions—language, nationality, measurement systems, building methods and codes, etc.—less divisive. It makes the foreign familiar. By contrast, current interest in regionalism and tradition suggests a reaction to this condition. See: *Architectureproduction*, ed. Beatriz Colomina (New York: Princeton Architectural Press, 1988).

THE LANDSCAPE OF MEMORY

17. Lampugnani, "Architectural Exhibitions," 30-55.
18. Walter Benjamin, "A Berlin Chronicle," reprinted in *Reflections* (New York: Schocken, 1986) 8-9.
19. Kleihues, *Schriftenreihe zur Insternationalen Bauausstellung*, 69.
20. For example, between July and October of 1927 the Weißenhof Siedlung was open to the public and drew over 20,000 visitors on peak days. During the summer of 1957 the Hansaviertel (though only partially complete) averaged 12,000 daily viewers. See Barbara Lane Miller, *Architecture and Politics in Germany 1918-1945* (Cambridge: Harvard University Press, 1968), 122 and Lampugnani, "Architectural Exhibitions," 78-81.
21. Pierre-Alain Croset, "The Narration of Architecture" in *Architectureproduction*, 203-205.
22. Susan Sontag, *On Photography* (New York: Farrar, Strauss & Giroux, 1973), 157. See also John Berger, "Uses of Photography" in *About Looking* (New York: Pantheon, 1980), 64-80.
23. Sontag, *On Photography*, 20.
24. Lampugnani, "Architectural Exhibitions." Recently, Lampugnani has reflected on the IBA's goals and accomplishments in "Il 'caso' Berlino: tentativo di un bilancio di sette anni di lavoro," *Domus* (1988).
25. Indeed, some would argue this lack is a function of present day Germany by claiming that architects are a reflection of their society or nation. The German Democratic Republic and the Federal Republic of Germany were relatively young countries (founded in 1949) "artificially" created by, and closely affiliated to, outside powers. See Goerd Peschken, "Bei Kaffee und Grappa," in *Architekturlehre*, ed. Philip Oswalt, (Berlin: Symposium AG/Symposium der streikenden Architekturstudent Innen/T.U. Berlin, 1989): 65-67.
26. Christa Wolf, "A Model of Experience—A Discussion on *A Model Childhood*," *The Fourth Dimension: Interviews with Christa Wolf*, (London: Verso, 1988), 51.
27. Teufelsberg ("Devils Mountain") is a "fake," made of rubble carted from buildings destroyed in World War II. It is sited on the ruins of Hitler and Speer's planned military academy.
28. Christa Wolf, *A Model Childhood* (London: Virago, 1988), 3.
29. Walter Abish, *Wie Deutsch Ist Es?* (New York: New Directions, 1979), 248-52.
30. Bernhard Schulz, "Der Errinerung Form Geben," *Der Tagesspiegel* (November 4, 1988), my translation.
31. Andreas Huyssen, "The Politics of Identification: 'Holocaust' and West German Drama" in *After the Great Divide* (Bloomington: Indiana University Press, 1986), 94-114.

James Turrell, "Fumerole walkway with solar and lunar alignments," Drawing for Roden Crater, Arizona, with photographic emulsion, graphite, and conte crayon on mylar, 1983.

In mythic origins, the first human place was the sky, made by Jove's thunder and lightning. To see it more clearly, the primeval forest was cleared; the clearings or "eyes," loci, became groves as centers for ritual. These swidden clearings were the fields for the first agricultural practices. The place-making rituals and geometry of the clearing were later transferred to foundation rites. Out of the great variety of practices connected to such clearings came the many now-strange associations connecting such diverse topics and places as theater, temple, forum, sacrifice, trial, labyrinth, and chorus. The first mythic clearings established the site both as the embodiment of the sacred and as the source of human culture. If thought proper is seen to consist of the power to make reflected distinctions, then one could regard the site as the first generative result.[1]

CAROL J. BURNS

ON SITE:
ARCHITECTURAL PREOCCUPATIONS

In architectural design, the demands of relating a building to a physical location are necessary and inevitable; the site is initially construed and finally achieved in the architectural work. The problems attendant to siting have a pervasive and profound impact on buildings. Nonetheless, architectural theory and criticism have tended to address siting issues with descriptive or analytic references to specific exemplary projects. This approach exclusively reveals through circumstantial strategies the lack of a clear conceptual basis for the notion of site within architecture.[2] Because of its intrinsic importance and generative potential, the conceptual content of site must be made available for study and opened to question as a means to disclose and, ultimately, to challenge the motives and precepts of the discipline.

I suggest a twofold consideration of the site in architecture: in terms of theory or knowledge (what we think site is), and in terms of the impact of theory on action (what we make of a site, or how it informs constructions and is formed through them). This emphasis on thought and action poses fundamental questions: What is a site? How is it constructed? And how can a site inform building and architecture? These obvious but remarkably resistant questions stem from a conviction that architecture is not constituted of buildings or sites but arises from the studied relationship of the two and from an awareness that site is received as an architectural construct, even if unconsciously. Historically the notions of site and architecture have shifted from the sacred to the profane (churches to institutions), from the specific to the general (premodern to modern), and from the unique to the nostalgic (prototype to type). Considering the site in terms of theory and siting in terms of architectural activity outlines the insistent intersections of architecture, site, and construction and also illuminates design thinking in architecture. The topic here is not simply the site; it is equally the architectural understanding of the site. This inquiry is comprised of a survey of the changing status of site, certain applications of the concept, and a reading of the terms by which site is construed. It is meant to be suggestive, not exhaustive.

The emergence of "site" as a concern in areas other than architecture underscores its importance to theoretical constructions in economics, politics, and sociocultural conditions. The term's nuance has been expanded by its appropriation in divergent discourses, although, as Desa Philippi has noted, it has not been given definition in these disciplines: "[This] is signalled by the ubiquity of the notion of site across the discourses that constitute the domains of knowledge in the Western World, from sociology to philosophy, from political science to the arts... Indeed, 'site' threatens to become a free floating signifier, attaching itself to an astounding number of objects: the artwork has become a site itself rather than existing in relation to one; the body is a site; as are even its organs."[3] The text is called a site, so are discourses. Texts are constructs, and discourses are contexts in which texts are read; site applies to both, indicating its simultaneous and multiple scales of reference.

The present status of site as a shaping force within architecture is a reaction to the mainstream ideology of modern architecture. Called "the International Style" or "functional modernism," the names given to modern architecture betray a concern for universalizing issues unrelated—even opposed—to those arising from the specificity of a given place. Motivated by technological developments, the possibility of producing widely available quality goods, and a social program with utopian aspirations, the modernist program in conjunction with a developing global economy led to standardization of environments and cultures. Reactions against the resulting widespread homogeneity are evident in diverse architectural responses of the last twenty years: attempts by environmental planners to search out and involve local community groups in decision-making processes; the identification of specific practices within defined geographic or cultural locales (for example, the Ticino or Southern California); academic ideologies based on methodological response to specific built contexts (such as the Cornell school); and the articulation of a theory of regionalism in architecture.[4] Vittorio Gregotti summarizes the arguments this way: "The worst enemy of modern architecture is the idea of space considered solely in terms of its economic and technical exigencies indifferent to the idea of the site."[5] Admittedly, the concern for site is only one of the reactive developments that have become initiatory, contributing to widespread alteration in the perceived hierarchy of forces shaping architecture today. As the awareness of the relationship between cultural production and the local circumstances of material practice has come to the fore, attention to site has begun to frame the problem of making and interpreting architecture.

At present, site is frequently seen as a synchronic phenomenon, irrevocably divorced from other times. The history of a setting is acknowledged only insofar as the forces acting upon it have affected its present visible form. " 'Site' has come to mark a particular conjunction where the temporal is eroded by the spatial and where history becomes the isolated image of its residue."[6] However, local circumstances cannot be considered simply in terms of space; they also require a diachronic apprehension of time. As Kurt Forster has said, "No understanding of a site is conceivable without a communal history, or conceivable with a substitution of that history . . . We may very well suffer from a curious historical impatience. The expectation that meaning can be generated instantaneously seems to have become, partly, a surrogate subject of contemporary projects."[7] Traditionally, the exclusive object of site planning is space; the potential to plan or "plot" time is not pursued. The principle of the (so-called) master plan is to design the space of a terrain over an extended time; there must exist a similar, perhaps paradoxical, potential for plotting the time of a terrain over space, which would differ from an architectural narrative or promenade by specifically accounting for growth and change in time.

ARCHITECTURAL PREOCCUPATIONS
THE CLEARED SITE / THE CONSTRUCTED SITE
In order to focus on the site within architectural thinking, two opposed conceptions (resulting from the reactive processes outlined above and representing positions that have currency) will be examined: the cleared site and the constructed site.

The idea of the cleared site is based on an assumption that the site as received is unoccupied, lacking any prior constructions and empty of content. It posits space as objective and "pure," a neutral mathematical object. This assumed neutrality fosters the impression that the land and the space of a site are independent of political motive.[8] This attitude prevails most strongly over undeveloped land, which is perceived as void of architectural context even though

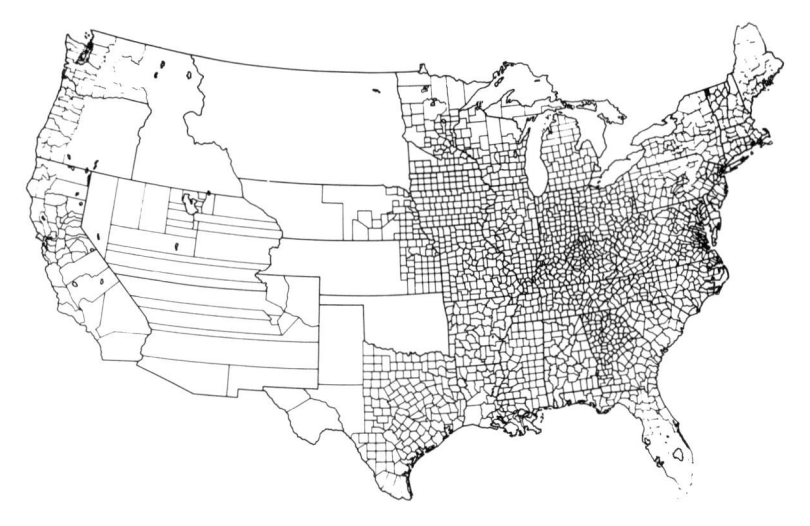

County boundaries of the United States, 1860, Line drawing

replete with natural constructions—vegetation, drainage systems, wind patterns, animal habitats, and so forth. Natural constructions are considered secondary to human constructions by architecture and the planning disciplines; only landscape architecture recognizes their status insofar as the disciplinary means and methods are developed around them. The disregard for natural constructions betrays the presumption that they are politically and ideologically immaterial. The cleared site conception, which is apparently nonpolitical and nonideological, implies that the mechanisms adapted by the planning disciplines are equally neutral in ideological terms, equally unengaged with issues of power. As a stratagem, it offers great latitude by fostering an illusion that planning is apolitical.

The cleared site argument depends on the mathematicization of land, a technique fundamental to the basic comprehension of the environment. "In Western societies the first step toward control of an environment usually is the assigning of tracts as grants of property—done by drawing lines on paper, although little may be known about the tract that is to be colonized."[9] To rationalize land is to objectify it profoundly. For example, the so-called Jeffersonian grid—inspired by precedents as old as Ptolemy's map and centuriation, the Roman system of land division—has been applied to 69 percent of the land in 48 American states. Taken for granted and generally accepted as an advantage for settlement, its application was explicitly motivated by economic and governmental control: "Congressional townships of thirty-six miles were created by federal law for the sole purpose of making available easily identifiable and saleable tracts... The Land Ordinance Act of 1785 [has divided land] into rectangles of sections and townships by whose lines the settler has been able easily and certainly to locate his farm and the forester his forty. In the local organization of the Middle West these lines have played an important part."[10] The pervasive presence of the federal rectangular grid has rendered it, for most Americans and Canadians, inevitable or even natural. Nevertheless, the grid has the effect of making real differences in sites invisible; it presumes equal access to all land; and it denies specificity to each parcel. As an embodiment of the human effort to conquer space, surveying has enormous impact on the understanding of land use, the perception of landscape, and the ensuing land development; it shapes the outline and content of any piece of land available as a location for architecture. Far from being objective or neutral, geometry and mathematics are constructions that occupy sites.

When applied to land, the abstract clarity of geometry becomes "invisible."[11] The rationalism that objectifies the site via geometry masks itself by virtue of its uniformity and masks the site's topographical irregularities, flattening the land and the perception of the land. Ernst Cassirer has said:

> Cognition devises symbolic concepts—the concepts of space and time [and geometry]—in order to dominate the world of sensory experience and survey it as a world ordered by law, but nothing in the sensory data themselves immediately corresponds to [the symbolic concepts] . . . The logic of things cannot be separated from the logic of signs. For the sign is no mere accidental cloak of the idea, but its necessary and essential organ . . . No form of cultural activity can develop its appropriate and peculiar type of comprehension and configuration without, as it were, creating a definite sensuous substratum for itself. This substratum is so essential that it sometimes seems to constitute the entire content, the true 'meaning' of these forms."[12]

Geometry, laid over land, providing it with content, is one such substratum. Invisible and immaterial, it cannot be extracted from land because it emplaces and encloses the land: one cannot divorce the site from the way it is known.

The technique of the cleared site depends on the map and the plan, organizational constructs that help to level the ground, presenting it as a supporting platform or foundation of no important matter. The debased ground plane is abstracted so that ensuing planning operations may introduce content to the cleared site. For the architecture of the cleared site, buildings form that content—visible superstructures imported onto and overriding the demoted terrain.

Mies van der Rohe, Project for Chicago Convention Center, photo collage, 1939

The most notable designs founded on the cleared site are of a scale massive enough to clear and rebuild the setting literally. Projects conceived on a podium—such as United Nations Plaza, Albany Government Center, or the Acropolis—convey the requisite power to claim, "flatten," and build powerful sites. However, the ensuing architecture need not carry such weight symbolically or literally; residential structures, the most commonplace of architectural commissions, without programmatic "weight," can also use the cleared site to convey monumentality. Mies van der Rohe's large urban complexes on Lake Shore Drive in Chicago and Westmount Square in Montreal place buildings with ideal plans into contradictory city fabrics, which are rendered ideal by clearing the immediate premises. The Farnsworth House, elevated above the high-water mark in a flood plain periodically cleared by nature, is built on land that might be considered "unbuildable" were it not for the strategy of the cleared site.

Such clearing, conveying self-expression and the "heroic" perception of the modern architect as artist, attempts to conquer a territory completely in a single effort, precluding change, development, and all future planning. In aiming to determine definitively the life of the place, the cleared site strategy undertakes to isolate architecture from time. The past is denied and the future is deemed powerless to change the situation, much less improve it. Denying any relationship to existing conditions, the architecture of the cleared site presumes a power to initiate and finalize the site in both spatial and temporal terms.

However, a real site cannot be removed from human time. The space of the site is made by humans and is by necessity political; any piece of land subject to human attention becomes charged with power and its mechanisms. This is the meaning or content that

Terraced hillslopes of surface mine, Appalachian Mountains, aerial photograph

humans bring to nature, that architecture must bring to the site. The cleared site exists only in eternity. It is a fantastic, poetic, or mythical character, a fiction invented by humans for the conquest of space and time. By presuming to arrest time and condemn physicality, the cleared site tries to deny its origin in human construction; it is a veiled attempt to remove itself from the human condition.

Opposed to the idea of the cleared site is that of the constructed site, which emphasizes the visible physicality, morphological qualities, and existing conditions of land and architecture. Connecting the earth as natural form to the building as constructed form, the notion of the constructed site implies that the resulting architecture is meant to be understood in physical terms—building and setting are seen to be shaped through obviously physical processes.

The constructed site argument depends on the visible layers of landscape phenomena: first, the prehuman or prehistoric landforms resulting from chthonic forces; second, that which remains of the efforts and projects of the period when agriculture was dominant, in other words, rural landscapes, districts, and regions; third, a layer of transformations that occurred primarily during the industrial period, including increased settlement densities afforded by the invention of transportation systems such as railroads and canals; and, finally, the present processes, which are more diffuse but of a

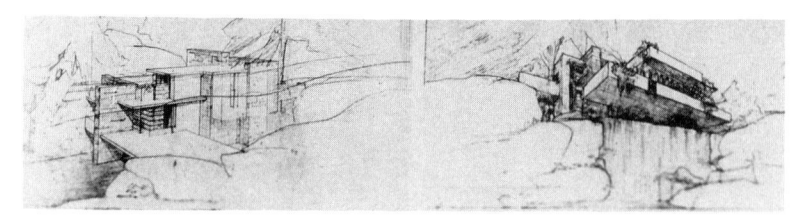

Frank Lloyd Wright, Edgar J. Kaufmann House ("Fallingwater"), Bear Run, Pennsylvania, Perspective, 1936

larger scale of operation and include, for example, highway systems and suburban and exurban development. These natural and human forces have shaped land, and any situation available for building has already been somehow physically constructed by these agencies.

Though these layers are constituted of physical material (in contrast to mathematical abstractions) they are also difficult to see. The layers, accumulated over time, are not seen as distinct strata, nor do their phenomena appear as discrete. They are visually obscure because they are physically and spatially coextensive, which leads to interruption, simultaneity, discontinuity, synchronism, fragmentation, coincidence, and disruption; they cohere only in abrupt juxtapositions. As the abstract overlay of mathematics masks topography by systematizing it, the physical phenomena, in apparently incoherent conjunction, effectively mask the systems—natural and man-made—that determine their present form.

The technique of the constructed site depends on the section as a composite device. Conveying the topographic qualities of both building and setting in the base line, the horizon line, and the profile line, the section also presents the visual character of the vertical surfaces beyond. It shows the visual construction of the setting in phenomenological terms and the conceptual or structural use of the visiblesetting in design thinking.

The method of the constructed site singles out particular visible phenomena to provide a generative concept, which is then used as a literal basis of construction. Several opportunities are lost in this approach. By valuing visible material, what is not immediately present is not addressed (for example, the history or the poetics of a place). The architecture devised for the spot is conceived as a constructive extension of the conditions of the location itself; it thus provides a further construction of the already constructed site. Though it may mediate between the landscape and the building, such architecture uses the site for its own support and extension. Therefore, though the situation is seen as generative, it is not intentionally shaped or designed by the architect; it is simply appropriated. But because building architecture necessarily entails building a site, even this apparently passive appropriation necessarily changes the situation. Therefore, rather than attempt to maintain a neutral stance, the architect must take responsibility for the site and assume its control for a limited passage of time.

Conceptions of the site—cleared and constructed—can be compared to certain attitudes about designing an addition to an existing work of architecture or construction.[13] One strategy for addition is the extension, which hides the new work by reproducing the forms and materials of the existing structure. As a pure strategy, this is obviously impossible in thinking about architecture as an addition to the (already constructed) site because the physical requirements of architecture are not satisfied by the forms of materials in nature. The other obvious strategy for addition is to design the new without relation to the existing structure as analogous to the model of the cleared site, which brings imported content to a situation conceived as without meaning. Yet another possibility is to investigate the existing situation—building, city, or native land—to discover its latent qualities or potential; inherent conditions can motivate the ensuing construction so that the new participates in the existing. This allows both a criticism and a release from the received conditions and, reciprocally, a reverberation of them so that the boundaries between the conditions as received and as renovated become blurred; both may be productive because both are aggressive with respect to each other.

In arguing that a site, as a result of human action, is always already conceptually and physically constructed prior to building architecture—which is to say, preoccupied by the way it is known and by its history—the apparent opposition of the cleared site and the constructed site are thrown into question. The site as received is never cleared or empty; indeed, it is not possible for the architect to clear the site of its own constituent formal content. Therefore, a cleared site model reveals itself to be a strategy for adding over and against the received site. The cleared site and constructed site are thus only ostensibly opposed. By denying or erasing the site, and by reducing its physical and temporal dimensions through a limited appropriation, the cleared site and the constructed site circumscribe the productive potential of the site.

ARCHITECTURAL PREOCCUPATIONS: CONSTRUING COMMON LANGUAGE

In every series of real terms, not only do the terms themselves and their associations and environments change, but we change, and their meaning for us changes, so that new kinds of sameness and types of causations continually come into view and appeal to our interest. —William James[14]

As commonly used, the word "site" means the local position of a building, town, monument, or similar work; it may also signify a space of ground occupied or to be occupied by a building; more generally, it describes the place or scene of something.[15] The term approaches some architectural characteristics in colloquial use—it is inclusive in scale (encompassing both the building and the town) and is explicitly associated with the position of three-dimensional constructs. Derived from verbs stressing action (*sinere*, meaning to leave, place, or lay; and *serere*, meaning to sow), a site results from human agency.

The architectural site eludes precise definition partly because of the disarming immediacy of its physical setting, which all too easily eclipses apprehension of its constructive and constitutive aspects. The initial approach to understanding site through some models and strategies within architecture is now followed through citation of its own meanings, the diverse denomination by which it is described in common language. Briefly, each term is taken in itself and to derive a suggestion as to how its understanding may illuminate or be brought into architectural thought and practice. This is to try to open to study the conceptual possibilities of the site in its own potential, not as a contingency to architecture but in its own multivalence.

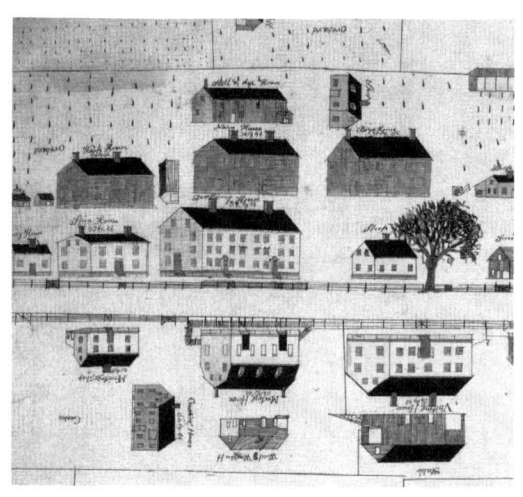

Brother Joshua Bussell, Map of Church Family Shaker Village, Alfred, Maine, Line drawing with color

The "lot" is a measured parcel of land with fixed boundaries as designated on a plot or survey. By association, it is simultaneously a fortune and a duty (to "draw lots" is to be subject to an operation of chance). The word also conveys contradictory meanings with respect to amount or measure: a lot is a fraction or a portion of some larger thing, as in a share; yet it is also a quantity significant in itself, as in "a lot of something." In architecture the term "lot" seems neutral. A person may buy a lot on which to build a house, but the location for the house is determined by ascribing values to certain aspects of the lot—orientation, setback, view, etc. The lot exists "prior" to the site and conveys only boundary and measure. However, boundary is a function of both legal and economic power, and measure is a function of knowledge. Thus, the apparently neutral term "lot" is situated at the intersection of knowledge and power, potent forces preoccupying the architectural site.

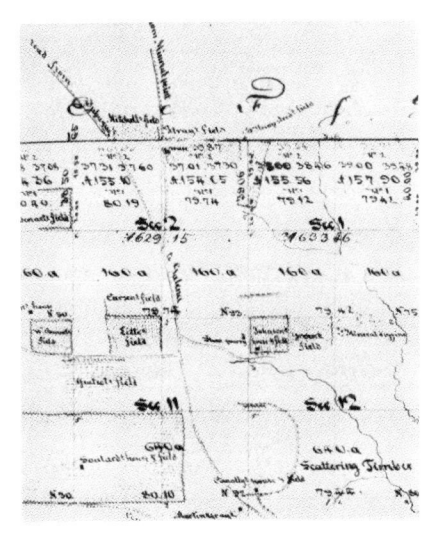

Northeast corner of West Galena Township plat, 1932-33, legal description

"Plot," like "lot," is an ancient word with consistent precise use and many different accompanying connotations. Most simply, plot is a measured piece of land. It is also a small area of planted ground; a graphic representation, as in a chart; and the outline of a literary work. The act of plotting implies careful foresight and intrigue, as in a devious plan. (Deviousness typically insinuates underhandedness or evil, though its strict derivation simply means "off the main road.") A plot is similar to a scheme in that each is a systematic plan, a representation of some type, and also devious in connotation. Thus, the plot at once demarcates the piece of land for a building, represents the land, and conveys the intended plan of action for change: to plot is to scheme is to design. Architectural design is by definition a "plot," a plan of positive action intending to promote change as a deviation from given reality. Each small area of measured land reveals the constructively deviant character of architectural thought.

Section 3, Arlington National Cemetary, photograph

A particular building or site is characterized at a scale larger than itself as being within a particular "context," a word widely used in architecture. Context literally means the "connection of words" and is defined as "the parts of a discourse that surround a word or passage and can throw light on its meaning." Local context is a topical concern in current architecture where, in contrast to the literary suggestion, it is implemented as generator, something that provides meaning or content in itself. In architecture context is broadly synonymous with environment. Both exist in relation to scale—a local context may have a specificity at odds with a larger regional context. Both are also subject to change over time—buildings around a site may be erected and demolished; a new building changes its own site and also changes its own larger context. The content of context—its constituent aspects and their ascribed values—is relative: one person may see construction materials as important; another individual may value the relationship of built parts over their material nature; a public agency may be concerned with context only as described by zoning, bulk, or setback rules. In architectural design, context is also subject to changes in representational—and conceptual—means. For example, context as seen in a figure/ground diagram stems from a spatial conception introduced by the Nolli map; the ongoing technological developments in cartography encourage different visual perceptions of context at different scales. Finally, context may not be exclusively visual—cultural context situates human efforts, and for architecture this includes, but is not circumscribed by, physical and spatial constructs.

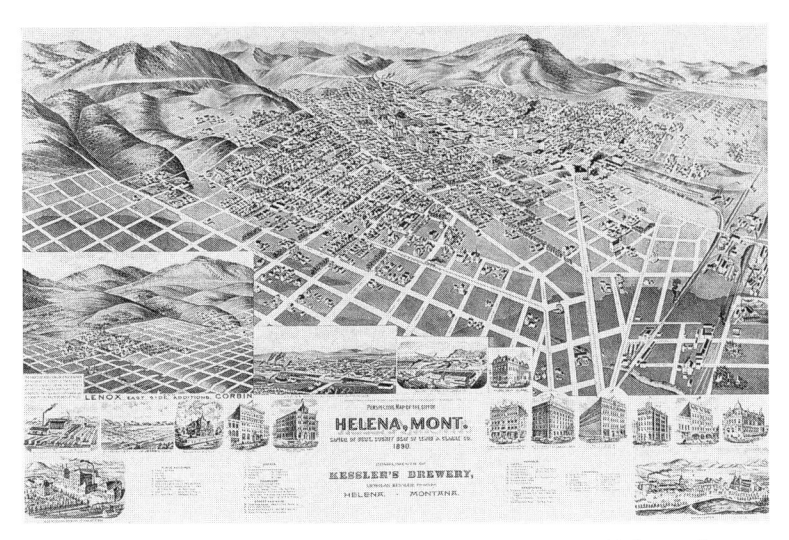

Perspective map of the City of Helena, Montana, unsigned toned lithograph

The concept of the "region" has provided a means of analyzing and promoting tendencies opposed to the homogenizing forces of modernism's "International Style." Ironically, the region is by definition "a broadly homogeneous or indefinite geographical area." The region can only be described indefinitely in dimensional or perceptual terms because geographical boundaries are often physically imprecise (for example, the Shenandoah Valley is topographically inseparable from the surrounding Appalachian Mountains) even if they limit or circumscribe movement (the mountains have a confining effect). The stabilizing of settlement sponsors the emergence of cultural distinctions from within different geographic regions; therefore, the region can be seen as the product of the interaction between geography and culture. Given the instability of the population today, the ease of transportation across natural boundaries, and a culture fueled by mass media, such interaction between geography and culture does not necessarily occur spontaneously, but depends on intentional effort. The derivation of region stems from the Latin *regere*, meaning "to rule," recalling the precise relationship between the land and the power of the ruler or king. Today, we must choose to be ruled by the region. The architectural implications of this term underline the power of political and ideological control in shaping physical areas.

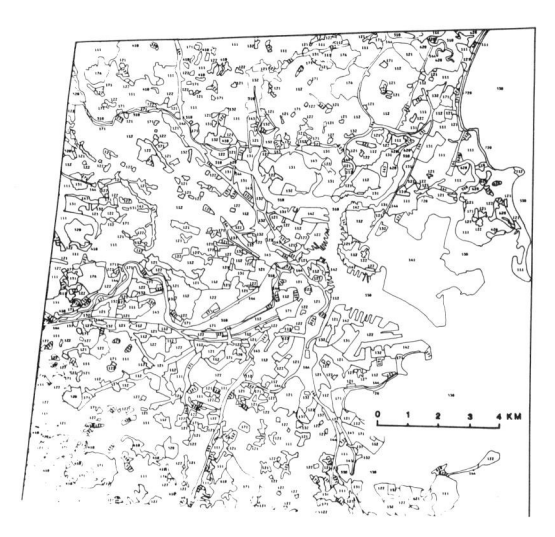

Portion of urban land-use and land-cover map of Boston compiled by satellite at 1:25,000 scale and produced by the Department of Forestry and Wildlife Management, 1990

Perception itself gives rise to the term "landscape," which literally means the portion of land that the eye can comprehend in a single view. A word of relatively recent origin, it stems from eighteenth-century concerns for the visible and the picturesque. The force of viewing is likewise felt in the word "survey," which in etymology means "to look over," and in definition means "to delineate extent and position by measurement." These two terms point out the difference between the "aesthetic" and "mathematic" conceptions of the site, yet each reflects and contributes to a distancing between the individual—or society—and land; this distancing has an economic basis in industrialization. The aesthetic and mathematic conceptions are also analogous to the tension between art and science in contributing to and determining architecture.

Emerson points out that aesthetic and mathematical conceptions are fundamentally different but intimately bound to one another:

The charming landscape which I saw this morning is indubitably made up of some twenty or thirty farms. Miller owns this field, Locke that, and Manning the woodland beyond. But

Art Sinsabaugh, "Landscape No. 64," photograph

ON SITE

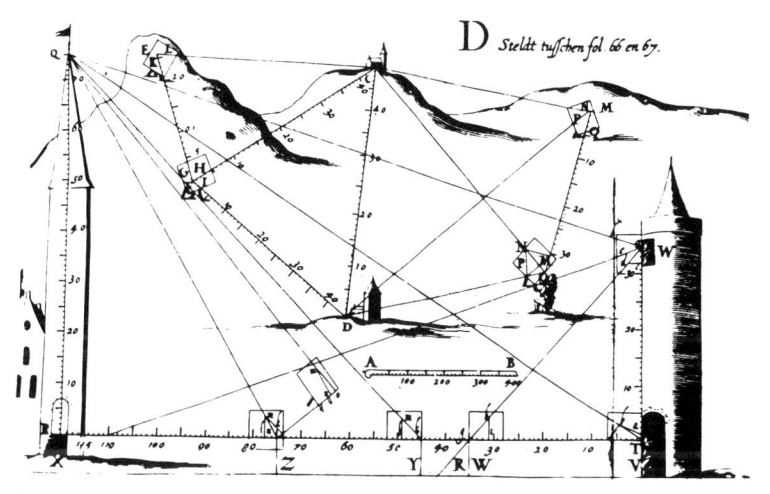

A means of applying the method of triangulation, graphic table

none of them owns the landscape. There is a property in the horizon which no man has but he whose eye can integrate all the parts, that is, the poet. This is the best part of these men's farms, yet this their warranty deeds give no title.[16]

Landscape and survey inform ways of seeing because they are forms of knowledge. Like architecture, they frame information or content; they control by establishing principles that make the world comprehensible.

Willard Dixon, "Mondrian with Cows," oil painting

Fort Union on the Santa Fe Trail, aerial photograph

The broad notion of placement underlies the terms "location" and "position." Their derivation from the Latin verbs *locare* and *ponere*, meaning "to place," bespeaks their applicability to circumstances including but not limited to buildings or constructs. The force of these general words within architecture is not to be underestimated (even within the maxims of real estate, the three most important criteria of property are reputedly location, location, and location). The local is defined as "not broad or general; characterized by, relating to, or occupying a particular place." Its root word, *locus*, has the nearly mathematical definition of "the set of all points whose location is determined by stated conditions." Without precise technical application to architecture, the Latin source of "local" is in "stall," suggesting some attributes of architectural siting: one sense of "stall" is that of a physical compartment, a space marked off; another is temporal, that of bringing to a standstill or delaying in time. Such stalling is embodied in architecture, most directly in the stela, a commemorative slab or pillar intentionally sustaining a moment in time in an enduring physical form. By extension, to locate or to site any construction is to mark off and delay the architecture and the site both spatially and temporally.

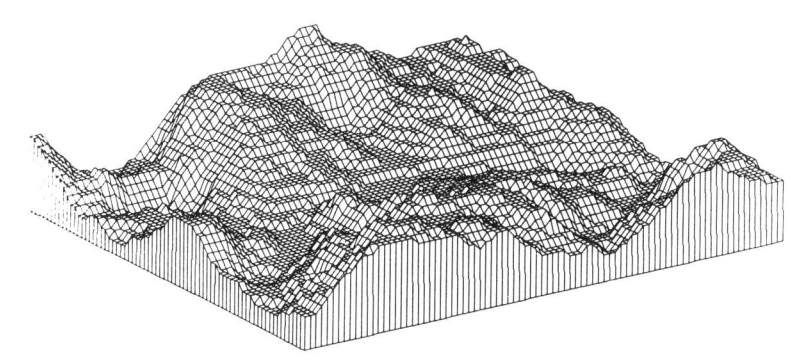

North Georgia, Wireframe perspective generated by automatic stereocorrelation of data taken by remote sensing, 1989

"Position" denotes the point or area occupied by a physical object. In physical terms it implies a site. "Position" derives from "positive," so that it also implies an advocacy, as, for example, in arguing a proposition or making a proposal. Taking a position implicates affirmation: having an idea is fundamentally affirmative; the making of an idea is the making of the place of the idea. Henri LeFebvre goes so far as to insist on the utopian quality of any idea: "Today more than ever, there are no ideas without a utopia . . . There is no idea which neither explores a possibility nor tries to discover a direction . . . The architects, like the town planners, know this perfectly well."[17] Position, as the location of an idea or architectural construction, affirmatively asserts the connection between place and ideology.

Reviewing these terms reveals the elastic nature of the breadth and scale of site semantically, experientially, and temporally. The "architectural" character of the site is suggested in the consistent motives of politics and logic, latent ideologies under apparent neutrality, which inform and are imbedded in the architectural site and are revealed when approached from unrelated, even opposing, viewpoints. Each approach to site has its own specificity, and through association each speaks to a particular understanding of architecture. It is the gaps between the terms, the overlaps and inconsistencies among them, that finally betray the nature of the architectural site as both inclusive and evasive. In their multiplicity and disjunction the words associated with the general notion of site bespeak the relative impossibility of defining the specifically architectural site.

The understanding of site is neither self-evident in looking at a particular example nor explicit in theoretical terms.[18] Every site is a unique intersection of land, climate, production, and circulation. Peirce Lewis has stated that "most objects in the landscape—although they convey all kinds of 'messages'—do not convey those messages in any obvious way."[19] The condition of each individual site makes its understanding in relation to the notion of site extremely difficult. Ernst Cassirer describes this as a basic noetic problem: "It is, as it were, the fundamental principle of cognition that the universal can be perceived only in the particular, while the particular can be thought only in reference to the universal."[20] The problematic reciprocity of the universal and particular speaks to architectural thinking and making. Though the architect's practical task is always specific to its circumstances, architecture as a discipline theorizes such tasks in general terms. In practical response to the complexity of the whole, designers attempt to reduce the site by seizing its particular aspects. This is exemplified by the constructed site's emphasis on the visible and by the cleared site's preference for the abstract. Architectural reductions of site, these conceptions implicate architectural practice.

Any site is already constructed by its specific circumstances. Adding a new building to a site transforms its use as well as its topography, microclimate, and circulation. The construction of a building defines successive sites for ensuing constructions—that is, any building alters adjoining sites as well as its own. The site is neither pure nor ideal; it is "claimed," which is to say it is preoccupied, by knowledge and power and time. As the embodiment and inscription of these preoccupations, the site is made in the work of architecture and is necessary if the work of architecture is to be made.

The site is a work, a human or social trace. It is comparable to a myth, temple, or city in that it is open to archeological deciphering. The site is a significative system with no singular author. Using nature to convey ideology, the site is a social product. The natural environment, long understood simply as a technical problem to be conquered, is now seen as threatened with destruction. However, like architecture, the environment and the site can also be created, molded, and transformed. The face of the earth, the landscape, and the site are products of human efforts. The site is also an economic product, and sites can be likened to "merchandise" in that there are interrelationships between the production of goods and that of the environment: the former accrues to groups who appropriate sites in order to manage or exploit them. John Locke theorized that land has no value without labor and that its value increases with the progress of settlement.

Settlement patterns are visual statements on the land that can be deciphered. Such a functional reading, however, fails to reveal the genetic aspect that brought the site into being. A complete assessment of the site must exist at several levels: the site can be described formally; critical analysis can define how and according to what methods the site was produced, including the crucial junctures of land use determination; finally, the real site must be analyzed, in other words, one must look at the people using the site, who perhaps are opposed to its physical form and purpose.

The apparent neutrality of the site—linked to the lack of comprehensive assessment—is a mask for issues of control. The discipline of architecture avoids admitting or taking responsibility for control and denies such power in relation to site. To attempt to detach the building from the site, in practice and theory alike, is to deny that any work of architecture is a work of site, to suppress that the work is political, ideological, and temporal, and to forget that it is implicated in the history of architecture.

In closing, it must be acknowledged that these remarks are both generally broad and specifically limited. They do not outline future work but suggest its potential. There are latent assumptions here to be challenged. For example,the persistent consideration of site as existing solely at or above the surface of the earth, the bias toward native rather than urban sites, or the apparent impossibility of a site in "wilderness" all argue for the need to qualify different kinds or types of sites. Because the topic of site initially seemed bounded or finite, it also seemed to be part of the discipline of architecture. However, in concluding that the means of thinking site is a means of thinking architecture, it ends by enveloping the discipline.

Though the site is a product of culture, it is by nature not a finished or closed product. It is an artefact of human work that can neither be completed nor abandoned. Its meaning can never be determinable. The site, like the human condition, is open. This is the surplus of site, its indefinable excess.

The Great Plains, aerial photograph

"No totality can be meaningful in any case, except a finished one (a historical humanism, an intellectual object, a book, some other product of écriture), which can only be a part of our present totality and which necessarily has a closed structure, whereas the 'structurality' of [the human] situation . . . is open."[21]

ON SITE

1. Paraphrased from Donald Kunze, *Thought and Place* (New York: Peter Lang Publishing, 1987), 124.
2. Two noteworthy sources in art theory have potential relevance to architecture. Robert Irwin, in *Being and Circumstance* (San Francisco: The Lapis Press, 1985) delimits four categories of built works in terms of their relation to site: site dominant, site adjusted, site specific, and site conditioned. Rosalind Krauss, in "Sculpture in the Expanded Field," first published in *October* 8 (Spring 1979) locates sculpture in a "logically expanded field" established by the binary pairing of architecture and landscape.
3. Desa Phillipi, "Invisible Sites," *Sight Works Volume One: Several Enquiries* (London: Chance Books, 1988).
4. See Kenneth Frampton, "Towards A Critical Regionalism: Six Points for an Architecture of Resistance," *The Anti-Aesthetic*, ed. Hal Foster (Seattle: Bay Press, 1983).
5. Vittorio Gregotti, "Lecture at the Architectural League," *section a*, vol.1, no. 1 (March 1983), 8.
6. Phillipi, *Sight Works*.
7. Kurt Forster, *Site: The Meaning of Place in Art and Architecture*, ed. Mildred Friedman in *Design Quarterly*, no.122 (Cambridge: MIT Press, 1983), 27.
8. See Henri LeFebvre, "The Politics of Space," *Antipode*, vol.8, no.2 (May, 1976), 31.
9. Hildegard Binder Johnson, *Order Upon the Land* (New York: Oxford University Press, 1976), 21.
10. Johnson, *Order Upon the Land*, 116.
11. For a discussion of the relation of geometry, mapping, and landscape representation in land reclamation and the settlement of the Veneto, see Denis Cosgrove, "The Geometry of Landscape: Practical and Speculative Arts in Sixteenth-Century Venetian Land Territories," ed. D. Cosgrove and S. Daniels in *The Iconography of Landscape* (Cambridge: Cambridge University Press, 1988).
12. Ernst Cassirer, *The Philosophy of Symbolic Forms*, Vol.1: *Language* (New Haven: Yale University Press, 1955), 86.
13. This discussion of the addition was originally set out with respect to the work of Frank Gehry in my essay, "The Gehry Phenomenon," in *Thinking the Present: Recent American Architecture* (New York: Princeton Architectural Press, 1990), 72-88.
14. William James, "On the Notion of Reality as Changing," in *A Pluralistic Universe* (Cambridge: Harvard University Press, 1977).
15. *Webster's Seventh New Collegiate Dictionary* (Springfield: Merriam Co., 1970).
16. As cited by Johnson in *Order Upon the Land*, frontispiece.
17. LeFebvre, "The Politics of Space," 35.
18. This points to the paradox that it is necessary to approach site, which is a non-discursive construct, through language. In fact, this paradox underlies all writing about architecture.
19. F. Peirce Lewis, "Axioms for Reading the Landscape," *The Interpretation of Ordinary Landscapes*, ed. D.W. Meinig (New York: Oxford University Press, 1979), 19.
20. Cassirer, *The Philosophy of Symbolic Forms*, 86.
21. Caws, Peter, "Structuralism," *The History of Ideas*, ed. Philip P. Weiner, (New York: Charles Scribner's Sons, 1973), 329.

LOIS E. NESBITT

POSTSCRIPT

An editor engaged in "a practice of architectural theory and criticism" asks a number of writers to transform architecture by devising new ways of thinking and writing about the discipline. The lives and pursuits of these women are themselves a challenge to the discipline: most write and teach as well as build, reflecting a desire to reshape things for the long haul, to influence minds and not just dazzle eyes, to change the way we think as well as what we see.

And to what end? To open things up, to reveal what has been suppressed, to question unquestioned assumptions, fixed distinctions, seamless systems. To shake this discipline of architecture to its foundations—and from there to unearth and analyze those foundations like archaeologists at an old, old site.

The result—this book—a series of scrappy, sometimes disjunctive texts, from Peggy Deamer's fragments to the associative web that Jennifer Bloomer weaves around the disappearing center of a Piranesi drawing; texts as strings of quotations; oppressively allusive texts; texts that obsessively dissect the meanings of the words that they employ, exploring and in some cases inventing etymologies (Burns's essay as a glossary of dissolving and disintegrating terms). In short, *difficult reading*.

In an essay itself stitched together from heterogeneous genres—allegory, narrative, exposition, criticism—Virginia Woolf discussed the plight of contemporary writers of fiction: the "tools" inherited from the past were outdated, obsolete, simply useless. "For us, those conventions are ruin, those tools are death," and so with the current generation "the smashing and the crashing began ... Grammar is violated, syntax disintegrated,"[1] and the great, awkward, unprecedented masterpieces of Joyce, Eliot, and the others came into being.

The writers of the present volume face a similar problem, and their texts too bear the markings of smashing and crashing. Broad-ranging, scattered allusions challenge even the most versatile reader. These writers borrow, steal, pillage, wrest the Promethean fire from Foucault, Lacan, Joyce, Pynchon, Plato, Alberti, and others, but the borrowing is selective, the reuse subversive; the father, as Bloomer acknowledges, is deliberately *misread*. The conventions, even those of the most recent and most sophisticated theories, are in ruins, the tools are not right for the job. Yet this odd melange, this cacophony of partially obliterated languages is the closest thing that we have to a common language, to "conventions." And, as Woolf points out, conventions are necessary to discourse—unless the writer "puts before [the reader] something which he recognizes," there is no common springboard from which to leap into the unknown. So Joyce fashioned *Ulysses* from the shards of an inverted *Odyssey*; so the writers here scavenge the past for what is worth salvaging. They selfishly and irresponsibly misread the fathers, disrupt the old ways of thinking, in order to ignite controversy but more importantly to fuel the dialogue across disciplines and between past and present.

And so these texts crisscross from literature to philosophy to classics to visual arts, revealing an impressive and intimidating erudition that leaves one feeling ignorant, inadequate. And this is the point: Refusing to accept the appalling intellectual and imaginative restrictiveness, the self-imposed isolation of the architect in his studio, these writers offer cross-fertilization, open exchange, a free-for-all. To do so they manoeuvre in the interstices, the places between, the cracks and gaps in which architecture by its very nature has always been forced to operate, and ask that we acknowledge the contradictions and complexities of these less determinate zones, that we not retreat behind the walls of (illusory) enclosures.

Moreover, these writers demand that we lift the veils of self serving ideology and rhetoric, that we not be blinded by sight. Mary Pepchinski designs an invisible monument for a community long anaesthetized to the visual traces of the Holocaust; Andrea Kahn argues that the dissimulated power structuring the Crystal Palace is far more insidious than the overt authoritarianism of Bentham's Panopticon; Anne Bergren destabilizes the order-restoring male gaze in order to continually reveal what has been repressed; Bloomer

---

1. All quotations are from Virginia Woolf, "Mr. Bennett and Mrs. Brown" (1924).

slices multiple sections through conflicting realities; Miriam Gusevich dissects the self-perpetuating forces that keep the canon intact; Deamer, analyzing erotically charged male texts, illustrates that (visual) perception is never neutral.

A large part of this re-vision, of course, is aimed at the blind spots of modernism—its ahistoricism, its claims to universality, its coercive social agenda cloaked in the irreproachable guise of utopianism. What has been passed off as universal, "natural," and permanent must now be seen for what it is: particular, man-made, and malleable—be it the actual built environment or the mental framework shaping that environment. The body, oddly absent figure in architectural discourse, also makes an aggressive reappearance here, not as a Renaissance ideal or a Corbusian modular man mechanically inscribed in the measured geometry of a draftsman's universe but as a living, breathing, desiring organism. From the sexual friction of Deamer's critics to the wildly proliferating vaginal imagery of Bloomer's fertile prose to Ingraham's fleshed-out line, latent and/or illicit sexuality and physicality intrude on architecture's chilly abstractions. And in so doing they reveal needs, desires, and fantasies—of conquest and seduction and finally of power—long transmuted into and concealed under a facade of detachment and objectivity. Architecture *lives* in these pages, and this coming to life of the inanimate realm that we have long believed to be under our control is itself nerving. What emerges by necessity in this unsettled time lacks grace, finesse, polish. To quote Woolf again:

> For these reasons, then, we must reconcile ourselves to a season of failure and fragments. We must reflect that where so much strength is spent on finding a way of telling the truth, the truth itself is bound to reach us in rather an exhausted and chaotic condition . . . It is the sound of their axes we hear.

Perhaps it is now time to put down the books, pens, note cards and ask what *is* going on out in the field—something not addressed directly by most of these authors. *Are* changes occurring? If so, where? Or where may we expect them to occur? And what form will they take? And how might *we* participate? In the spirit of this collection, this is intended less as a tidy endnote, less as a postscript than as a provocation. Let us not be afraid to smash and crash, but let us also dare to erect new structures—lopsided, incomplete, and unbalanced but through whose ample cracks and seams the breath of life—inspiration—can once again pass.

Figure Credits

Deamer

p. 26	Bruno Balestrini; from Roland Martin, *Greek Architecture* (New York: Electa/Rizzoli, 1980).
p. 28	Foto Mairani; from Martin, *Greek Architecture*.
p. 30	Heinrich Wölfflin, *Principles of Art History*, trans. M. D. Hottinger (New York: Dover, 1950).
p. 32	*John Ruskin: An Arts Council Exhibition* (London: Publications Department Arts Council of Great Britain, 1983).
p. 34	Alinari, Florence; in H. W. Janson, *History of Art* (Englewood Cliffs, NJ: Prentice-Hall, 1962).
p. 36	Adrian Stokes, *The Critical Writings of Adrian Stokes*, vol. 2 (London: Thames and Hudson, 1978).

Bloomer

p. 57	Courtesy of the Cooper-Hewitt Museum, Smithsonian Institution/Art Resource NY. Gift of Eleanor and Sarah Hewitt, 1931-94-71. Photo: Ken Pelka.

Ingraham

p. 65	*Carlo Scarpa: Architecture in Details* (Cambridge: MIT Press), 1988.
p. 68.	*Alexander World Atlas* (Stuttgart: Ernst Klett, 1990).

FIGURE CREDITS

p. 69   Catherine Ingraham.
p. 70   Brenda Richardson, *Barnett Newman, The Complete Drawings 1944-1969* (The Baltimore Museum of Art, 1979). Courtesy Annalee Newman insofar as her rights are concerned.
p. 75   *Imago Mundi: A Periodical Review of Early Cartography*, ed. Leo Bagrow (Stockholm: Harding and Curtis, Ltd., 1947).
p. 77   Mark Rosentahl, *Jonathan Borofsky's Modes of Working* (New York: Harry Abrams Inc.).

KAHN

pp. 87-91, 98   Georg Kohlmaier and Barna von Story, *Houses of Glass* (Cambridge: MIT Press, 1986).
pp. 94t, 95   Loius K. Meisel, *Richard Estes: The Complete Paintings 1966-1985* (New York: Abrams, 1976).
p. 94b   "Playtime"; courtesy of Janus Films.
p. 100   Robin Evans, *The Fabrication of Virtue: English prison architecture, 1750-1840* (London: Cambridge University Press, 1982).

BERGREN

p. 109   Antiquarium, Berlin.
p. 110   Charles Eisen (ca. 1750) from La Fontaine, *Fables*.
p. 111   Catherine Millot, *Nobodaddy: L'hystérie dans le siècle* (Paris: Point hors ligne).
p. 115   Courtesy of Tim Street-Porter, Photographer.
pp. 116l, 117, 120b   Courtesy of Tim Bonner, Photographer.
p. 116r Courtesy of Morphosis.
p. 120t Courtesy of Morphosis.
pp. 121-123   Courtesy of John Whiteman.

PEPCHINSKI

All photographs by Mary Pepchinski.

BURNS

p. 146   William Nettles in Julia Brown, ed., *Occluded Front: James Turrell* (Los Angeles: The Lapis Press, 1985). Drawing in the collection of Robert and Mary Looker, Santa Barbara, California.
pp. 150, 157, 161b   Hildegard Binder Johnson, *Order Upon the Land* (New York: Oxford University Press, 1976). Painting p. 161b courtesy of William Sawyer Gallery, San Francisco.

FIGURE CREDITS

pp. 162, 166	William A. Garnett in Nathaniel Alexander Owings, *The American Aesthetic* (New York: Harper & Row, 1969).
p. 152	Mies van der Rohe.
p. 153	Denys Brunsden, *The Unquiet Landscape* (New York: Wiley, 1978).
p. 154	Alberto Izzo and Camillo Gubitosi, *Frank Lloyd Wright: Three quarters of a Century of Drawings* (New York: Horizon Press, 1981).
p. 156	*National Geographic* (September 1989).
p. 158	Harold Wise in Gene Gurney, *Arlington National Cemetary* (New York: Crown Publishers).
p. 159	John W. Reps, *Cities on Stone* (Fort Worth: Amon Carter Museum, 1976).
p. 160t	*Photogrammetric Engineering & Remote Sensing* (February, 1990).
p. 160b	Art Sinsabaugh in John Szarkowski, *The Photographer and the American Landscape* (New York: The Museum of Modern Art, 1963).
p. 161t	*Arte e Scienza per Il Designo del Mondo* (Milan: Electa, 1983).
p. 161b	Hildegard Binder Johnson, *Order Upon the Land* (New York: Oxford University Press, 1976).
p. 163	*Photogrammetric Engineering & Remote Sensing* (November, 1989).

AUTHORS' BIOGRAPHIES

Ann Bergren received a Ph.D. in Classical Philology from Harvard University. She has taught Classics at Princeton University and the University of California, Los Angeles, where she is an Associate Professor, and architectural theory at the Southern California Institute of Architecture. She is currently a fellow of the Chicago Institute for Architecture and Urbanism and writing a book, *Architecture Gender Philosophy: Programmata for an Architecture of Metis.*

Jennifer Bloomer teaches, writes about, and enjoys a minor practice of architecture. She is a Fellow of the Chicago Institute for Architecture and Urbanism, S.O.M. Foundation and author of *Desiring Architecture*, forthcoming from the Yale University Press. She is currently working on The Domesticity Project in collaboration with Catherine Ingraham and an architectural project which explores and extends the ideas of Louis Sullivan.

Carol J. Burns is Assistant Professor of Architecture at Harvard University Graduate School of Design and an architect with a practice in Connecticut. She graduated from the Yale School of Architecture, where she edited the journal *Perspecta* 21, which included The Norfolk Projects, site specific constructions by architects and sculptors.

Peggy Deamer, a practicing architect in New York City, has taught at Columbia University and Barnard College since 1983 and currently teaches at Princeton University. She received her B.A. from Oberlin College (1972), B.Arch from Cooper Union (1977) and Ph.D from Princeton University (1987) with a dissertation on Adrian Stokes. Her writings on theory and criticism have been published in various journals including *Assemblage*.

Miriam Gusevich was born in Havana, Cuba and received her B. Arch and M. Arch from Cornell University. She is a professor of design and theory and has taught at a number of schools, among them Columbia University, University of Wisconsin-Milwaukee, and University of Illinois, Chicago. Her writings have appeared in diverse journals, including *New German Critique, Discourse, Midgard,* and *Inland Architect.* Gusevich has been the recipient of various awards including the 1985 Arnold W. Brunner Grant (New York AIA) and a fellowship at the Center for 20th Century Studies (UW-M). She is currently Planning and Development Manager for the Chicago Park District where she designs and implements master plans throughout the city.

Catherine Ingraham is an Assistant Professor in the Department of Architecture at the University of Illinois, Chicago, and a Visiting Critic at Columbia University in New York. She has lectured and published extensively on architecture and architectural theory and has been a a Fellow at the Chicago Institute for Architecture and Urbanism (CIAU). Editor of *Restructuring Architectural Theory* (Northwestern University Press, 1989), Ingraham is working on a book entitled *The Burdens of Linearity: Architectural Constructions.* Her architectural projects include a theoretical design project for a library and a design project on domesticity.

Andrea Kahn is a New York architect engaged in a practice of architectural theory and criticism. Born in Montreal, Canada, she received a B.A. in Philosophy/Architecture from Bennington College and a M.Arch from Princeton University. She has taught design and theory at a variety of schools, including Columbia University, Bennington College, Carnegic-Mellon, and University of Cincinnati. Her writings have appeared in *Harvard Architectural Review, Journal of Architectural Education,* and *Design Book Review.*

Mary Pepchinski was born in Yonkers, New York. She received a B.A. from Barnard College, and a M.Arch from Columbia University in 1982. During the past decade she has exhibited architectural and sculptural projects in galleries and institutions in New York and West Berlin. Commentaries upon her work have appeared in *The New York Times, The Harvard Architectural Review, Interview, Metropolis, Gedenken und Denkmal,* and *Der Tagesspiegel.* Since 1987 she has lived in West Berlin where, since 1988, she has been a teaching assistant at the Technische Üniversität Berlin. She is a member of the Architektenkammers Berlin and Nordrhein-Westfalen.